Segregation of Duties (SOD) Policies in IAM

James Relington

DEDICATION

To those who seek knowledge, inspiration, and new perspectives—
may this book be a companion on your journey, a spark for curiosity,
and a reminder that every page turned is a step toward discovery.

AKNOWLEDGEMENTS

I would like to express my deepest gratitude to everyone who contributed to the creation of this book. To my colleagues and mentors, your insights and expertise have been invaluable. A special thank you to my family and friends for their unwavering support and encouragement throughout this journey.

Introduction to Segregation of Duties (SOD)

Segregation of Duties (SOD) is a fundamental principle in risk management and internal controls, particularly within the realm of Identity and Access Management (IAM). It is designed to prevent conflicts of interest, fraud, and errors by ensuring that no single individual has excessive control over critical business processes. The concept of SOD is based on the idea that tasks and responsibilities should be divided among multiple individuals or roles to minimize risk exposure and enhance security. By distributing responsibilities, organizations can mitigate threats related to unauthorized access, data breaches, and insider threats, which are increasingly prevalent in today's digital landscape.

The implementation of SOD policies in IAM is crucial for maintaining compliance with regulatory requirements and industry standards. Many laws and frameworks, such as the Sarbanes-Oxley Act (SOX), the General Data Protection Regulation (GDPR), and ISO 27001, emphasize the importance of controlling and monitoring access to sensitive information. Organizations that fail to implement adequate SOD measures risk financial penalties, reputational damage, and legal consequences. Regulatory bodies expect businesses to demonstrate robust access control mechanisms that prevent employees, contractors, or third parties from accumulating excessive privileges that could lead to security vulnerabilities.

IAM plays a central role in enforcing SOD by defining user roles, responsibilities, and access permissions within an organization. Identity management solutions help ensure that users only have the minimum level of access required to perform their job functions. This principle, known as the principle of least privilege (PoLP), is closely related to SOD, as it limits the ability of individuals to perform conflicting duties. When properly implemented, IAM systems enforce role-based access control (RBAC) and other security measures that prevent users from obtaining unauthorized permissions that could compromise security and operational integrity.

One of the primary challenges in implementing SOD is identifying and defining potential conflicts within business processes. Organizations must conduct thorough risk assessments to determine which combinations of access rights could lead to security threats or compliance violations. For example, in a financial institution, an employee who has the ability to both create and approve payments presents a significant fraud risk. To mitigate this, companies must separate these duties across multiple users, ensuring that no single individual can execute a complete high-risk transaction without oversight.

In modern IAM frameworks, technology plays a key role in automating SOD controls and monitoring access activities. Organizations use policy-based enforcement mechanisms to detect and prevent violations in real time. Access certification campaigns, periodic reviews, and automated policy enforcement ensure that SOD conflicts are continuously monitored and resolved. Advanced IAM solutions integrate with Security Information and Event Management (SIEM) systems, providing real-time alerts and audit trails that help security teams identify anomalies and suspicious behavior.

A well-structured SOD policy requires collaboration between different business units, security teams, and compliance officers. It is not solely a technical issue but also an organizational and procedural challenge. To be effective, SOD policies must be clearly defined, documented, and communicated across the organization. Employees should be educated on the importance of access controls and the potential risks associated with policy violations. Awareness training can help prevent employees from inadvertently requesting or granting access that could lead to conflicts.

Despite its benefits, enforcing SOD policies can present practical challenges, particularly in large organizations with complex structures. Managing SOD in a dynamic business environment where employees frequently change roles, departments, or responsibilities requires continuous oversight and adaptive policies. Role creep, where users gradually accumulate unnecessary privileges over time, is a common problem that organizations must address through regular access reviews and recertifications. Automated role management tools help mitigate this issue by revoking unnecessary permissions and ensuring that access rights remain aligned with job functions.

Another key aspect of SOD is its application in cloud environments, where traditional access control models may not be sufficient. As businesses migrate to cloud-based services and adopt hybrid IAM strategies, ensuring SOD compliance becomes more complex. Organizations must consider multi-cloud IAM strategies that enforce SOD policies across diverse platforms, including Software as a Service (SaaS) applications, Infrastructure as a Service (IaaS) environments, and on-premises systems. Cloud Identity Providers (IdPs) play a crucial role in centralizing authentication and authorization processes, enabling consistent enforcement of SOD policies.

The evolving nature of cybersecurity threats underscores the importance of continuously improving SOD policies. Cybercriminals and insider threats exploit weaknesses in access controls to gain unauthorized access to sensitive systems and data. Organizations must stay ahead of these threats by adopting advanced technologies such as Artificial Intelligence (AI) and Machine Learning (ML) to enhance access risk analysis and anomaly detection. AI-driven identity analytics can help identify patterns of suspicious activity and recommend proactive measures to strengthen SOD enforcement.

As organizations expand their digital ecosystems and integrate third-party vendors, managing SOD in external relationships becomes increasingly important. Third-party access poses a unique set of challenges, as vendors and contractors often require access to critical systems. Organizations must implement stringent access governance controls that limit third-party access to only necessary resources while maintaining oversight through continuous monitoring and auditing.

Ultimately, SOD is not just a security best practice but a business necessity for organizations that prioritize risk management, compliance, and operational integrity. A robust SOD framework strengthens an organization's ability to detect, prevent, and respond to access-related risks, ensuring that business processes remain secure and trustworthy. By leveraging IAM solutions, automated controls, and continuous monitoring, organizations can successfully implement SOD policies that align with regulatory expectations and industry standards.

The Importance of SOD in Identity and Access Management (IAM)

Segregation of Duties (SOD) is a crucial component of Identity and Access Management (IAM), serving as a foundational principle in maintaining security, compliance, and operational integrity within organizations. The primary goal of SOD is to ensure that no single individual has excessive control over critical business functions, thereby reducing the risk of fraud, errors, and unauthorized access. By distributing responsibilities among different users or roles, organizations can create checks and balances that protect sensitive information and critical systems from internal and external threats.

In the context of IAM, SOD plays a vital role in defining access rights and permissions across various enterprise applications, databases, and IT systems. Without proper enforcement of SOD, an individual could accumulate excessive privileges that enable them to manipulate financial transactions, alter critical data, or bypass security controls. This poses significant risks, particularly in industries such as finance, healthcare, and government, where regulatory compliance and data protection are paramount. By ensuring that conflicting duties are assigned to separate individuals, SOD helps organizations uphold the integrity of their business operations while maintaining adherence to regulatory requirements.

One of the most compelling reasons for implementing SOD in IAM is its effectiveness in preventing fraud and malicious activity. When employees or system administrators have unrestricted access to key processes, the likelihood of fraudulent behavior increases. For example, in financial systems, an individual who has the authority to both initiate and approve payments can exploit this privilege for personal gain. Similarly, in IT environments, a system administrator with unrestricted access to user accounts and security settings could manipulate logs to conceal unauthorized activities. SOD mitigates these risks by requiring multiple levels of approval, ensuring that no single user has unchecked control over critical operations.

Compliance with legal and regulatory frameworks is another essential reason why SOD is integral to IAM. Various industry standards and regulations mandate strict access control measures to protect sensitive data and prevent security breaches. Regulations such as the Sarbanes-Oxley Act (SOX), the General Data Protection Regulation (GDPR), and the Health Insurance Portability and Accountability Act (HIPAA) all emphasize the need for well-defined access controls and segregation of duties. Organizations that fail to enforce SOD policies risk severe financial penalties, reputational damage, and potential legal consequences. Implementing SOD not only helps businesses comply with these regulations but also demonstrates a commitment to cybersecurity best practices and risk management.

IAM solutions provide a structured framework for enforcing SOD policies across an organization's digital infrastructure. Role-based access control (RBAC) and attribute-based access control (ABAC) are commonly used IAM models that facilitate SOD enforcement. RBAC assigns permissions based on predefined roles, ensuring that users only have access to the resources necessary for their job functions. ABAC, on the other hand, incorporates contextual attributes such as location, time, and device type to determine access rights dynamically. By integrating these models into IAM strategies, organizations can automate SOD enforcement, reducing the risk of access conflicts while improving overall security posture.

The process of implementing SOD in IAM requires a comprehensive understanding of business processes and potential risks. Organizations must first identify areas where conflicting access rights could lead to security vulnerabilities. This involves mapping out key business functions and determining which roles or responsibilities should remain separate to prevent conflicts of interest. For example, in procurement systems, the individual responsible for approving purchase orders should not be the same person who processes payments. Similarly, in HR systems, an employee with access to payroll data should not have the ability to modify employee records without oversight. By defining these access controls, organizations can establish a clear framework for SOD enforcement.

Continuous monitoring and auditing are essential to maintaining effective SOD policies. IAM solutions provide automated tools for tracking access permissions, detecting policy violations, and generating audit reports. Regular access reviews help organizations identify users who may have accumulated conflicting privileges over time, a phenomenon known as role creep. By periodically reviewing access rights and removing unnecessary permissions, organizations can ensure that SOD policies remain effective in mitigating security risks. Furthermore, IAM systems with built-in analytics and artificial intelligence capabilities can proactively identify unusual access patterns, enabling security teams to respond to potential threats before they escalate.

Despite its benefits, enforcing SOD in IAM presents challenges, particularly in large and dynamic organizations. Employees frequently change roles, departments, or job functions, requiring continuous updates to access controls. Traditional IAM systems that rely on manual processes struggle to keep up with these changes, leading to access conflicts and compliance gaps. To address this challenge, organizations leverage automated IAM solutions that streamline role management and policy enforcement. Modern IAM platforms integrate with enterprise resource planning (ERP) systems, human resource management systems (HRMS), and cloud applications to ensure seamless synchronization of user roles and access rights.

The shift towards cloud computing and remote work has further complicated SOD enforcement in IAM. As organizations adopt cloud-based services and hybrid IT environments, managing access across multiple platforms becomes increasingly complex. Cloud Identity Providers (IdPs) play a critical role in maintaining centralized authentication and access management, enabling organizations to enforce SOD policies consistently across on-premises and cloud environments. Identity federation and single sign-on (SSO) solutions also help improve security by reducing the need for multiple credentials while maintaining strict access controls.

Another key aspect of SOD in IAM is managing third-party access. Many organizations rely on external vendors, contractors, and partners who require access to corporate systems. Without proper oversight, third-party users may gain excessive privileges that violate SOD policies, increasing the risk of data breaches and compliance violations. Organizations must implement strict access governance measures, such as just-in-time (JIT) access provisioning and zero-trust security frameworks, to ensure that third-party access is granted only when necessary and is revoked promptly when no longer needed.

The growing reliance on artificial intelligence and machine learning in IAM has introduced new opportunities for improving SOD enforcement. AI-driven identity analytics can assess access risks in real time, providing security teams with actionable insights to mitigate potential conflicts. Machine learning algorithms can detect anomalous behavior, such as an employee attempting to access sensitive data outside of their usual work patterns, and trigger automated responses to prevent security incidents. By incorporating AI into IAM strategies, organizations can enhance their ability to enforce SOD policies dynamically and adapt to evolving threats.

Effective SOD enforcement requires collaboration between multiple stakeholders, including IT teams, security professionals, compliance officers, and business leaders. It is not solely an IT responsibility but a strategic initiative that impacts the entire organization. Clear communication, ongoing training, and awareness programs help employees understand the importance of SOD policies and their role in maintaining security. By fostering a security-conscious culture and leveraging advanced IAM technologies, organizations can build a resilient access control framework that safeguards their most critical assets.

Historical Evolution of SOD Policies

The concept of Segregation of Duties (SOD) has evolved significantly over time, shaped by historical events, regulatory developments, and advancements in technology. The principle of separating critical responsibilities to prevent fraud and errors dates back to ancient civilizations, where governance structures required multiple individuals to oversee financial transactions and decision-making processes. As societies developed complex economic and administrative systems, the necessity of internal controls and checks to prevent corruption became a fundamental aspect of governance and business operations. Over the centuries, SOD policies have been refined and formalized, eventually becoming a cornerstone of modern Identity and Access Management (IAM) frameworks.

The earliest forms of SOD can be traced back to ancient Mesopotamia, Egypt, and China, where centralized governments managed vast resources and trade networks. In Mesopotamian societies, financial transactions and taxation were recorded on clay tablets, with scribes assigned specific roles to ensure accuracy and accountability. The division of labor among tax collectors, auditors, and record-keepers prevented individuals from manipulating financial records for personal gain. Similarly, in ancient Egypt, temple priests and royal officials managed the collection and distribution of grain, ensuring that no single person had control over both the collection and storage of resources. This system of checks and balances laid the foundation for later financial and administrative controls.

During the Roman Empire, the concept of separation of duties became more structured, particularly in military and government administration. Roman law mandated that financial oversight be divided among different officials to prevent embezzlement and abuse of power. Treasurers, auditors, and magistrates were assigned distinct responsibilities, ensuring that financial transactions were reviewed by multiple individuals before approval. This system extended to the military, where procurement and logistics functions were managed separately from command decisions to minimize the risk of corruption. The principles established during this era influenced governance models in European kingdoms and early financial institutions.

With the expansion of global trade in the Middle Ages, financial accountability became increasingly important for merchant guilds and banking institutions. The rise of early banking systems in Venice, Florence, and other trade hubs led to the development of double-entry bookkeeping, a significant milestone in the evolution of financial controls. This accounting method, pioneered by Luca Pacioli in the late 15th century, introduced the principle of recording debits and credits separately, ensuring that financial records could not be easily manipulated. Double-entry bookkeeping reinforced the need for segregation of financial duties, requiring multiple individuals to validate transactions and maintain accurate records.

The Industrial Revolution marked a turning point in the evolution of SOD policies, as businesses grew in scale and complexity. Large manufacturing enterprises and financial institutions required structured internal controls to manage operations efficiently. The expansion of corporate structures introduced new risks, prompting companies to implement formalized policies to separate key business functions. This period saw the establishment of audit practices, where independent reviewers assessed financial statements and operational controls to detect fraud and mismanagement. As corporations became more complex, the need for structured governance frameworks became evident, leading to the development of early internal control models.

The 20th century brought significant advancements in regulatory oversight, reinforcing the importance of SOD in corporate governance. The stock market crash of 1929 and the ensuing Great Depression highlighted widespread financial fraud and mismanagement, prompting governments to introduce stricter regulations on financial reporting and internal controls. In the United States, the Securities Exchange Act of 1934 established the Securities and Exchange Commission (SEC) to oversee corporate disclosures and prevent fraudulent activities. This regulatory framework emphasized the necessity of independent audits and financial transparency, reinforcing the role of SOD in financial institutions and publicly traded companies.

In the latter half of the 20th century, the emergence of computerized systems transformed the way organizations implemented and enforced SOD policies. The widespread adoption of information technology introduced new risks related to data security and access management. Organizations began developing internal IT controls to ensure that no single employee had excessive privileges over critical systems. The rise of enterprise resource planning (ERP) systems, such as those developed by SAP and Oracle, required businesses to implement strict access controls to prevent unauthorized modifications to financial and operational data. As cyber threats increased, IT governance frameworks such as the COBIT (Control Objectives for Information and Related Technologies) model were introduced to help organizations manage risk and compliance.

The early 2000s saw a surge in regulatory reforms following high-profile corporate scandals, including the collapses of Enron and WorldCom. These incidents exposed significant weaknesses in internal controls, leading to the enactment of the Sarbanes-Oxley Act (SOX) in 2002. SOX introduced stringent requirements for financial reporting, internal controls, and corporate accountability, mandating that companies implement SOD policies to prevent fraudulent financial activities. Organizations were required to document and test their internal controls, ensuring that financial transactions were properly segregated and reviewed. The implementation of SOX marked a major milestone in the evolution of SOD, as businesses worldwide adopted more rigorous compliance measures to prevent corporate misconduct.

The rapid advancement of digital transformation in the 21st century has further shaped the evolution of SOD policies. The adoption of cloud computing, artificial intelligence, and automation has introduced new challenges in access control and identity management. Organizations must now enforce SOD policies across distributed environments, ensuring that users do not accumulate excessive privileges across multiple platforms. The rise of identity governance solutions has enabled businesses to automate access reviews, monitor user behavior, and enforce policy-based access controls. With regulatory frameworks such as the General Data Protection Regulation (GDPR) and the Payment Card Industry Data Security Standard (PCI DSS), businesses must maintain strict oversight of user access to protect sensitive data and ensure compliance with global standards.

Today, SOD policies continue to evolve in response to emerging security threats and regulatory requirements. Cybersecurity concerns, insider threats, and sophisticated attack methods have made SOD enforcement a critical aspect of risk management. Organizations are increasingly leveraging artificial intelligence and machine learning to analyze access patterns and detect potential violations in real time. The integration of zero-trust security principles further enhances SOD enforcement by continuously verifying user identities and restricting access based on dynamic risk assessments. As organizations continue to adopt digital technologies, the principles of SOD remain a fundamental component of safeguarding critical assets and ensuring operational integrity.

Throughout history, the evolution of SOD policies has been driven by the need for financial transparency, risk mitigation, and regulatory compliance. From ancient financial controls to modern IAM frameworks, the principles of separating critical duties and enforcing accountability have remained central to organizational security. As businesses navigate an increasingly digital and interconnected landscape, the ongoing refinement of SOD policies will continue to play a vital role in ensuring trust, security, and compliance across industries.

Key Principles of SOD Enforcement

The enforcement of Segregation of Duties (SOD) is a fundamental practice in organizational governance, security, and risk management. It ensures that no single individual has complete control over critical business functions, thereby reducing the risk of fraud, errors, and unauthorized actions. SOD is essential in Identity and Access Management (IAM), where access rights must be carefully controlled to prevent conflicts of interest and ensure accountability. Effective enforcement of SOD requires adherence to key principles that guide organizations in defining, implementing, and maintaining proper access controls across their systems and processes.

A fundamental principle of SOD enforcement is the clear separation of conflicting duties within an organization. This means that responsibilities for key processes should be divided among multiple individuals or teams to prevent any one person from executing an entire transaction without oversight. For example, in financial operations, the individual responsible for initiating a payment should not be the same person who approves or processes it. In IT systems, the administrator managing user accounts should not be the same person responsible for reviewing access logs. This separation prevents misuse of authority, intentional or accidental, and ensures that critical transactions are subject to checks and balances.

Another critical principle is the establishment of well-defined roles and access privileges. Role-based access control (RBAC) is a widely used approach that assigns users specific permissions based on their job functions. By structuring access rights around predefined roles, organizations can ensure that users only have the minimum level of access required to perform their duties. This approach reduces the risk of individuals accumulating excessive privileges over time, a phenomenon known as role creep. Regular reviews of user roles and access permissions help organizations maintain compliance with SOD policies and adapt to changing job responsibilities.

Enforcing SOD effectively requires a strong governance framework supported by documented policies and procedures. Organizations must clearly define SOD rules, specifying which duties must remain segregated and which combinations of access rights pose a risk. These policies should be integrated into IAM systems, ensuring that access controls are automatically enforced when users request new permissions. Governance structures should also include designated compliance officers or audit teams responsible for monitoring adherence to SOD policies and conducting periodic reviews to identify and address violations.

Risk-based assessment is another key principle in the enforcement of SOD. Not all business processes carry the same level of risk, so organizations must prioritize enforcement efforts based on the potential impact of SOD violations. High-risk functions, such as financial transactions, payroll processing, and system administration, require stricter controls compared to lower-risk activities. By identifying and categorizing risks, organizations can apply SOD enforcement where it is most critical, ensuring that resources are allocated efficiently while minimizing operational disruptions. Automated risk analysis tools can help organizations assess potential conflicts in user access and provide recommendations for mitigating risks.

The enforcement of SOD should be supported by continuous monitoring and auditing. Organizations must establish mechanisms to track user activity, detect policy violations, and generate audit reports. IAM solutions with built-in analytics and reporting capabilities enable organizations to identify suspicious behavior, such as unauthorized access attempts or deviations from standard workflows. Regular audits help organizations verify that SOD policies are being followed and provide an opportunity to refine access controls based on evolving business needs. Continuous monitoring ensures that SOD enforcement remains proactive rather than reactive, allowing organizations to detect and respond to security threats in real time.

Access request and approval workflows play a significant role in ensuring that SOD policies are enforced consistently. When users request access to critical systems or data, approval processes should involve multiple stakeholders, including managers, compliance teams, and system administrators. Automated workflows streamline the approval process while ensuring that access requests are properly reviewed before being granted. Implementing multi-factor authentication (MFA) and identity verification mechanisms further enhances security by ensuring that only authorized users can request and obtain access. Organizations should also enforce time-bound or temporary access for high-risk functions, ensuring that users receive permissions only for the duration required to complete a task.

Exception handling and remediation strategies are essential for maintaining the integrity of SOD policies. In some cases, business needs may require temporary violations of SOD rules, such as when an employee is on leave and a replacement must assume additional responsibilities. Organizations must have well-defined procedures for managing exceptions, including risk assessments, compensating controls, and documented approvals. Exception management should be tracked through IAM systems to ensure that temporary permissions are revoked once they are no longer needed. Additionally, organizations should implement remediation strategies to address recurring SOD violations and adjust policies as necessary to strengthen enforcement.

Training and awareness programs are crucial to the successful enforcement of SOD policies. Employees, managers, and administrators must understand the importance of SOD in preventing fraud, security breaches, and compliance violations. Regular training sessions and awareness campaigns help employees recognize potential conflicts of interest and understand their role in maintaining proper access controls. Organizations should also provide guidance on reporting SOD violations and encourage a culture of accountability where employees take responsibility for maintaining compliance with security policies.

The integration of artificial intelligence (AI) and machine learning (ML) in IAM systems is transforming the way SOD policies are enforced. AI-driven identity analytics can analyze user behavior patterns, detect anomalies, and provide real-time alerts for potential SOD violations. Machine learning algorithms can assess risk levels based on historical data and recommend preventive measures to strengthen enforcement. The use of AI in SOD enforcement enhances an organization's ability to adapt to evolving threats while reducing the burden on security teams. By leveraging advanced technologies, organizations can automate access risk analysis and improve the accuracy and efficiency of SOD enforcement.

Cloud computing and hybrid IT environments have introduced new challenges in enforcing SOD policies. Organizations must ensure that SOD principles are consistently applied across on-premises systems, cloud applications, and third-party services. The use of cloud identity providers (IdPs) and federated identity management helps organizations centralize authentication and access control, reducing the complexity of enforcing SOD across multiple platforms. Organizations should also implement least privilege access principles in cloud environments, ensuring that users do not accumulate excessive permissions beyond their required job functions. Regular audits of cloud access policies help maintain compliance with SOD enforcement in distributed environments.

As organizations continue to adopt digital transformation initiatives, the importance of effective SOD enforcement cannot be overstated. Cybersecurity threats, regulatory requirements, and evolving business models necessitate a proactive approach to managing access risks. By adhering to key principles such as role-based access control, continuous monitoring, risk-based assessment, and automation, organizations can strengthen their security posture while maintaining compliance with industry standards. The successful enforcement of SOD requires collaboration across departments, leveraging advanced IAM technologies, and fostering a culture of accountability to ensure that critical business functions remain secure and resilient.

Common Risks Addressed by SOD in IAM

Segregation of Duties (SOD) is a critical component of Identity and Access Management (IAM) that helps organizations mitigate a wide range of security, operational, and compliance risks. By ensuring that no single individual has excessive control over critical business processes, SOD reduces the likelihood of fraud, unauthorized access, data breaches, and regulatory violations. Without proper enforcement of SOD, organizations expose themselves to significant vulnerabilities that could lead to financial losses, reputational damage, and operational disruptions. The implementation of SOD policies within IAM frameworks directly addresses some of the most common risks faced by businesses across various industries.

One of the primary risks addressed by SOD is the potential for fraud and financial misconduct. When employees have unrestricted access to financial transactions, procurement systems, or payroll processing, they may exploit their privileges for personal gain. In cases where a single individual has the authority to both initiate and approve payments, the risk of fraudulent transactions increases significantly. SOD prevents such scenarios by requiring multiple approvals and independent oversight for financial operations. By enforcing access controls that separate duties related to fund transfers, expense approvals, and financial reporting, organizations can deter fraudulent behavior and maintain the integrity of their financial systems.

Unauthorized access to sensitive data is another major risk that SOD helps to mitigate. Many organizations store critical business information, intellectual property, and customer data in centralized systems that must be protected against insider threats and external attacks. Without proper access controls, employees may gain unauthorized access to confidential data, either intentionally or accidentally. SOD policies ensure that access to sensitive information is limited based on job roles, responsibilities, and security clearance levels. IAM solutions enforce these policies by restricting access to data repositories, requiring authentication and authorization before granting permissions, and logging all access attempts for audit purposes.

Insider threats pose a serious challenge to organizations, as employees with excessive privileges can manipulate systems for malicious purposes. Unlike external attackers, insiders already have legitimate access to enterprise systems, making it difficult to detect and prevent unauthorized activities. SOD minimizes insider threat risks by implementing strict access controls that limit the ability of employees to bypass security measures. By ensuring that no single individual has complete control over critical processes, organizations can reduce the likelihood of data theft, sabotage, or system manipulation. Monitoring user activity, enforcing least privilege access, and conducting regular access reviews further strengthen defenses against insider threats.

Data integrity risks are another concern that SOD addresses within IAM frameworks. When employees have unchecked access to modify, delete, or manipulate business-critical data, the accuracy and reliability of organizational records become compromised. This can lead to errors in financial statements, corrupted databases, or the loss of important transactional records. SOD policies prevent such risks by requiring dual approvals for data modifications and ensuring that individuals responsible for data entry are not the same individuals who verify or approve changes. IAM solutions reinforce these controls by tracking all modifications to sensitive data, generating alerts for unauthorized changes, and maintaining an audit trail for compliance purposes.

Non-compliance with industry regulations and legal requirements is a significant risk that SOD helps organizations address. Regulatory frameworks such as the Sarbanes-Oxley Act (SOX), the General Data Protection Regulation (GDPR), and the Health Insurance Portability and Accountability Act (HIPAA) mandate strict access control measures to protect financial data, personal information, and healthcare records. Organizations that fail to implement SOD policies risk facing severe penalties, legal actions, and reputational damage. IAM systems that enforce SOD enable businesses to meet compliance requirements by ensuring that access to regulated data and systems is properly segregated, monitored, and documented. Compliance audits and certifications further validate the effectiveness of these controls in preventing security breaches and regulatory violations.

Privilege escalation is another critical risk that SOD helps mitigate in IAM. In many cases, employees or system administrators may accumulate excessive privileges over time, either due to role changes, improper access provisioning, or insufficient oversight. This accumulation of privileges, often referred to as role creep, creates security vulnerabilities that attackers can exploit. If an employee with high-level access credentials falls victim to phishing or malware attacks, an adversary can leverage their privileges to gain unauthorized access to critical systems. SOD prevents privilege escalation by enforcing role-based access controls, regularly reviewing user permissions, and implementing automated access revocation mechanisms. By limiting the scope of user access and preventing the accumulation of excessive privileges, organizations can reduce the risk of security breaches and system compromise.

Conflicts of interest in business operations are another risk that SOD policies help to address. In organizations where employees are responsible for multiple functions, there is a potential for conflicts that can lead to unethical decision-making and financial mismanagement. For example, in procurement departments, an employee who has the authority to approve vendor contracts should not be responsible for making payments to those vendors. Similarly, in human resources, an individual processing payroll should not have the ability to create or modify employee records without independent oversight. SOD eliminates these conflicts by ensuring that high-risk functions are segregated and subject to multi-level approvals. IAM solutions automate these controls by enforcing policy-based access restrictions that prevent individuals from assuming conflicting roles.

Operational inefficiencies and lack of accountability are additional risks that SOD enforcement helps mitigate. When employees have broad access to systems and processes without proper segregation, accountability for actions becomes unclear. If a security incident, data breach, or system failure occurs, it becomes challenging to determine responsibility and implement corrective measures. SOD improves accountability by assigning specific roles and responsibilities to different individuals, ensuring that actions can be traced back to authorized users. IAM systems enhance this process by maintaining detailed logs of user activity, generating reports for security teams, and integrating with forensic analysis tools to investigate suspicious behavior.

Compromised system security due to excessive administrative access is a growing concern in IAM, particularly in cloud environments and hybrid IT infrastructures. Many organizations rely on privileged access management (PAM) solutions to control administrative access to servers, databases, and network resources. Without proper enforcement of SOD, privileged users may have unrestricted access to perform critical system modifications, increasing the risk of misconfigurations, security lapses, and unauthorized system changes. SOD reduces this risk by implementing least privilege principles, requiring just-in-time access provisioning, and enforcing approval workflows for administrative actions. Multi-factor authentication (MFA) and session monitoring further enhance security by ensuring that privileged users operate within predefined constraints.

As organizations continue to expand their digital footprints, the risks associated with identity and access management become increasingly complex. Cyber threats, regulatory pressures, and evolving business models require a proactive approach to SOD enforcement to safeguard critical assets. By addressing fraud, unauthorized access, insider threats, data integrity risks, compliance violations, privilege escalation, conflicts of interest, operational inefficiencies, and compromised system security, SOD policies serve as a foundational element of risk management in IAM. Organizations that effectively enforce SOD controls can strengthen their security posture, improve regulatory compliance, and maintain the trust of their stakeholders in an increasingly interconnected digital landscape.

Regulatory Requirements for SOD Compliance

Segregation of Duties (SOD) is not only a best practice in Identity and Access Management (IAM) but also a mandatory requirement in many regulatory frameworks worldwide. Governments and industry bodies have established strict compliance standards to ensure that organizations implement SOD controls to prevent fraud, unauthorized access, and security breaches. Regulatory requirements for SOD compliance vary by industry and jurisdiction, but they all share a common objective: enforcing internal controls that reduce the risk of financial misconduct, data breaches, and operational failures. Organizations that fail to comply with these requirements face significant penalties, reputational damage, and legal consequences, making SOD enforcement a crucial aspect of corporate governance and security management.

One of the most influential regulatory frameworks mandating SOD compliance is the Sarbanes-Oxley Act (SOX), enacted in 2002 in response to major corporate scandals such as Enron and WorldCom. SOX requires publicly traded companies in the United States to implement internal controls over financial reporting to ensure accuracy, transparency, and accountability. Section 404 of SOX specifically mandates that companies establish, document, and test internal control mechanisms to prevent financial fraud. SOD plays a critical role in meeting SOX requirements by ensuring that no single individual has unchecked authority over financial transactions. Organizations subject to SOX must conduct regular audits to verify that financial duties are properly segregated and that access controls are enforced to prevent unauthorized modifications to financial records. Failure to comply with SOX can result in heavy fines, loss of investor confidence, and potential legal actions against company executives.

The General Data Protection Regulation (GDPR), which governs data privacy in the European Union, also includes SOD as a critical compliance requirement. GDPR mandates that organizations handling personal data implement appropriate technical and organizational measures to protect sensitive information. This includes enforcing strict access controls and ensuring that employees only have access to the data necessary for their job functions. SOD policies help organizations meet GDPR compliance by preventing unauthorized data access and reducing the risk of insider threats. Organizations must demonstrate that they have proper mechanisms in place to restrict and monitor access to personal data, ensuring that sensitive information is not exposed to unauthorized personnel. Violations of GDPR can lead to significant financial penalties, with fines reaching up to four percent of an organization's annual global revenue.

The Health Insurance Portability and Accountability Act (HIPAA) is another regulatory framework that emphasizes SOD enforcement, particularly in the healthcare industry. HIPAA requires healthcare providers, insurers, and their business associates to protect the confidentiality, integrity, and availability of patient health information. Under the Security Rule, covered entities must implement administrative safeguards to prevent unauthorized access to electronic protected health information (ePHI). SOD policies are essential in HIPAA compliance, ensuring that healthcare employees do not have unrestricted access to patient records and that security-sensitive duties, such as system administration and data access, are properly separated. By enforcing SOD, healthcare organizations can minimize the risk of data breaches, medical fraud, and compliance violations, ultimately protecting patient privacy and maintaining regulatory adherence.

Financial institutions must comply with the Basel II and Basel III frameworks, which set global standards for risk management and banking regulations. These frameworks emphasize the need for strong internal controls, including SOD, to mitigate financial and operational risks. Banks and financial institutions must implement strict access control measures to prevent unauthorized transactions and ensure that critical banking functions are segregated among different personnel. Regulatory bodies such as the Federal Reserve, the Office of the Comptroller of the Currency (OCC), and the European Banking Authority (EBA) require financial institutions to conduct regular audits, perform risk assessments, and enforce access controls to comply with these regulations. SOD is a key element in preventing fraud, insider trading, and financial mismanagement in the banking sector, making it a mandatory requirement for institutions operating under Basel regulations.

The Payment Card Industry Data Security Standard (PCI DSS) enforces SOD compliance to protect credit card transactions and prevent fraud. PCI DSS applies to all businesses that process, store, or transmit credit card information, including retailers, financial institutions, and payment service providers. The standard requires organizations to implement strong access controls, ensuring that individuals handling cardholder data do not have overlapping responsibilities that could lead to fraudulent activities. Organizations must enforce role-based access control (RBAC), restrict administrative privileges, and implement multi-factor authentication to comply with PCI DSS requirements. Regular audits and penetration testing are also required to identify potential vulnerabilities and verify that SOD policies are effectively enforced. Failure to comply with PCI DSS can result in fines, increased transaction fees, and potential loss of the ability to process credit card payments.

Government agencies and defense contractors operating under the Federal Information Security Management Act (FISMA) and the National Institute of Standards and Technology (NIST) guidelines must also enforce SOD policies to secure sensitive government data. FISMA mandates that federal agencies and organizations handling government contracts implement strict security controls, including identity and access management measures that enforce SOD. NIST Special Publication 800-53 outlines access control requirements that ensure no individual has excessive privileges over classified or sensitive information. Organizations working with government entities must adhere to these requirements to maintain compliance with federal security standards and prevent unauthorized access to critical national security systems.

In addition to industry-specific regulations, organizations operating globally must navigate multiple regional compliance requirements that mandate SOD enforcement. The ISO 27001 standard for information security management systems (ISMS) includes specific controls related to access management and segregation of duties. ISO 27001-certified organizations must demonstrate that they have established processes to manage user access, prevent unauthorized actions, and enforce role-based security policies. Compliance with ISO 27001 helps organizations enhance their security posture while ensuring regulatory alignment across international markets.

Cloud computing and digital transformation have introduced new regulatory challenges, requiring organizations to extend SOD enforcement to cloud-based environments. The Cloud Security Alliance (CSA) and other industry groups have developed security frameworks that emphasize the importance of IAM controls, including SOD, in cloud governance. Organizations using cloud services must ensure that SOD principles are applied consistently across on-premises and cloud platforms, enforcing least privilege access and continuous monitoring. Regulatory bodies increasingly expect organizations to demonstrate that their SOD policies cover hybrid and multi-cloud environments, ensuring compliance with data protection laws and cybersecurity standards.

As regulatory requirements continue to evolve, organizations must adopt proactive measures to maintain compliance with SOD mandates. This includes automating access controls, conducting regular risk assessments, and integrating IAM solutions that enforce policy-based governance. Compliance teams must work closely with IT and security departments to ensure that SOD policies are consistently applied and that audit-ready documentation is maintained. By adhering to regulatory requirements for SOD compliance, organizations can strengthen their security posture, reduce financial and operational risks, and avoid costly penalties associated with non-compliance. The enforcement of SOD is not just a regulatory necessity but also a critical component of a comprehensive risk management strategy that protects business integrity, customer trust, and corporate reputation.

Designing an Effective SOD Policy Framework

An effective Segregation of Duties (SOD) policy framework is essential for organizations to prevent fraud, enhance security, and maintain compliance with regulatory requirements. SOD ensures that no single individual has complete control over critical business processes, thereby minimizing the risks associated with unauthorized access, financial mismanagement, and insider threats. Designing a robust SOD policy framework requires a strategic approach that aligns with an organization's operational structure, security objectives, and compliance obligations. To be effective, the framework must incorporate well-defined access controls, clear role definitions, risk assessments, and continuous monitoring mechanisms.

The first step in designing an SOD policy framework is to establish clear objectives that define the purpose and scope of segregation of duties within the organization. These objectives should align with business goals, regulatory requirements, and risk management strategies. Organizations must identify critical business processes that require segregation and determine the specific risks that SOD policies aim to mitigate. By defining the primary focus areas, organizations can ensure that their SOD policies address the most significant risks while supporting operational efficiency. The framework should also outline how SOD policies will be enforced, monitored, and updated as business needs evolve.

A fundamental component of an effective SOD framework is the identification of key business functions and the potential conflicts that may arise within them. Organizations must map out their operational workflows and determine where critical tasks should be segregated. Common high-risk areas include financial transactions, procurement, payroll processing, system administration, and data access management. For each business function, organizations must define the specific duties that need to be separated to prevent conflicts of interest. This process requires collaboration between business leaders, compliance teams, and IT security professionals to ensure that all critical functions are covered.

Role definition and access management play a crucial role in implementing an SOD framework. Organizations must establish well-defined roles and responsibilities for employees, ensuring that access rights are assigned based on job functions. Role-based access control (RBAC) is a widely used model that helps enforce SOD by restricting user permissions to the minimum necessary for performing job-related tasks. By structuring access controls around predefined roles, organizations can ensure that employees do not accumulate excessive privileges over time. In cases where attribute-based access control (ABAC) is used, organizations must incorporate contextual attributes such as department, location, or security clearance levels to refine access restrictions further.

Risk assessment is an essential step in designing an SOD policy framework. Organizations must evaluate potential risks associated with role combinations and identify scenarios where unauthorized actions could occur. Risk assessments should consider factors such as the likelihood of fraud, the impact of security breaches, and the potential financial and reputational consequences of policy violations. Using IAM solutions with automated risk analysis capabilities can help organizations detect conflicts in access rights and recommend corrective actions. By prioritizing high-risk areas, organizations can allocate resources more effectively and implement stricter controls where they are most needed.

Automation is a key element of a modern SOD policy framework. Manual enforcement of SOD policies is inefficient, error-prone, and difficult to scale, especially in large organizations with complex access management needs. IAM solutions provide automation capabilities that streamline access provisioning, role assignments, and policy enforcement. Automated workflows ensure that SOD policies are consistently applied across the organization, reducing the risk of human error and unauthorized access. Additionally, IAM systems enable organizations to conduct periodic access reviews and certification campaigns, ensuring that user permissions remain aligned with business requirements.

An effective SOD framework must include mechanisms for exception management. In certain situations, temporary policy exceptions may be necessary due to urgent business needs, personnel changes, or unforeseen circumstances. Organizations must establish clear procedures for requesting, approving, and documenting exceptions to SOD policies. Any temporary violation of SOD rules should be subject to additional oversight and compensating controls, such as requiring multiple levels of approval or implementing enhanced monitoring for high-risk activities. Exception handling should be logged in IAM systems, ensuring that deviations from SOD policies are tracked and reviewed periodically.

Continuous monitoring and auditing are critical for ensuring the effectiveness of an SOD framework. Organizations must implement real-time monitoring solutions that track user activity, detect policy violations, and generate audit logs for compliance reporting. Security teams should analyze access logs to identify unusual behavior, such as unauthorized privilege escalations or conflicting role assignments. Regular audits help organizations assess the effectiveness of their SOD policies and identify areas for improvement. By maintaining an audit trail of all access-related activities, organizations can demonstrate compliance with regulatory requirements and strengthen their security posture.

Employee training and awareness programs are essential components of a successful SOD framework. Employees must understand the importance of SOD policies, the risks associated with policy violations, and their role in maintaining compliance. Organizations should conduct regular training sessions to educate employees on access control best practices, role-based security principles, and procedures for reporting policy violations. Security awareness programs help foster a culture of accountability, ensuring that employees take responsibility for following access control policies and preventing conflicts of interest.

To ensure long-term effectiveness, organizations must continuously review and refine their SOD policy framework. Business processes, regulatory requirements, and security threats evolve over time, necessitating periodic updates to SOD policies. Organizations should conduct regular assessments of their access control strategies, incorporating feedback from security audits, risk assessments, and compliance reviews. As new technologies and IAM solutions emerge, organizations should explore opportunities to enhance their SOD enforcement capabilities through artificial intelligence, machine learning, and adaptive security models. By staying proactive and adaptive, organizations can ensure that their SOD framework remains effective in mitigating risks and maintaining compliance.

A well-designed SOD policy framework is essential for protecting organizations from fraud, security breaches, and regulatory violations. By defining clear objectives, identifying key business functions, enforcing role-based access controls, conducting risk assessments, leveraging automation, managing exceptions, implementing continuous monitoring, and educating employees, organizations can build a strong foundation for effective SOD enforcement. As security challenges continue to evolve, organizations must remain vigilant in maintaining and improving their SOD policies to ensure the integrity of their business operations and the protection of sensitive information.

Role-Based Access Control (RBAC) and SOD

Role-Based Access Control (RBAC) is a widely used access management model that simplifies the process of granting and revoking user permissions by assigning access rights based on predefined roles. RBAC plays a crucial role in enforcing Segregation of Duties (SOD) within an organization, ensuring that employees only have access to the resources necessary for their job functions while preventing conflicts of interest. By structuring access control policies around roles rather than individual users, organizations can implement SOD more effectively, reducing security risks, operational inefficiencies, and compliance violations.

RBAC operates on the principle that users are assigned to roles based on their responsibilities, and each role is associated with a specific set of permissions. This structured approach prevents individuals from accumulating excessive privileges, which could lead to unauthorized access, fraud, or data breaches. By enforcing least privilege access, RBAC ensures that employees cannot access functions beyond their job requirements, thereby reducing the risk of internal threats and accidental misconfigurations. SOD is directly supported by RBAC by ensuring that critical duties are assigned to separate roles, preventing any one person from having end-to-end control over sensitive business processes.

In an RBAC system, roles are defined based on business needs, departmental functions, and regulatory requirements. Organizations must carefully analyze their workflows to determine which duties need to be separated to maintain security and compliance. For example, in financial operations, the person responsible for initiating payments should not have the authority to approve them. In IT environments, a system administrator who manages user accounts should not be able to approve security changes without oversight. By mapping job functions to roles and enforcing these assignments through RBAC, organizations create a structured access control framework that aligns with SOD policies.

The implementation of RBAC requires a thorough analysis of role hierarchies and dependencies within an organization. Roles should be defined at multiple levels, from broad organizational roles to more granular function-specific roles. High-level roles may include general user access, managerial oversight, and administrative control, while more detailed roles may specify access to particular systems, databases, or applications. RBAC systems must also account for role inheritance, where higher-level roles inherit permissions from lower-level roles, ensuring that access control policies remain scalable and manageable. Organizations must carefully design their role hierarchies to avoid conflicts and prevent users from accumulating excessive privileges.

One of the key advantages of RBAC in enforcing SOD is its ability to prevent conflicting role assignments. Organizations must establish role conflict matrices to identify and mitigate potential SOD violations. A role conflict matrix defines which role combinations are prohibited to prevent employees from bypassing security controls. For example, an employee assigned to a role that allows data entry should not be granted a second role that permits data approval. By enforcing these constraints within RBAC systems, organizations can prevent unauthorized activities and ensure that SOD policies are consistently applied.

RBAC also supports the enforcement of access certification and periodic reviews, which are essential for maintaining compliance with SOD policies. Organizations must regularly review user role assignments to ensure that employees do not have unnecessary or conflicting access rights. Automated access reviews within RBAC systems allow security teams to identify anomalies, detect privilege escalations, and remove redundant permissions. By conducting routine role audits, organizations can maintain the integrity of their SOD framework and reduce the risk of security breaches resulting from outdated or misconfigured access rights.

Another important aspect of RBAC in relation to SOD is the concept of role lifecycle management. As employees change positions, get promoted, or move to different departments, their access needs evolve. Without proper role lifecycle management, users may retain privileges from previous roles, leading to role creep and SOD violations. Organizations must implement automated role provisioning and deprovisioning processes to ensure that access rights are updated in real-time based on job changes. Role-based onboarding and offboarding mechanisms help maintain security by ensuring that users only have access to the resources necessary for their current roles.

RBAC systems also enable organizations to enforce multi-factor authentication (MFA) and conditional access policies based on role sensitivity. Employees with access to critical functions or sensitive data may be required to provide additional authentication factors to verify their identity before performing high-risk actions. By integrating RBAC with adaptive authentication mechanisms, organizations can enhance security while maintaining compliance with SOD requirements. Conditional access policies can also restrict access based on contextual factors such as location, device, or network environment, ensuring that high-risk functions are protected from unauthorized access attempts.

In modern enterprise environments, RBAC must be extended to cloud-based applications, remote workforces, and third-party vendors. Traditional on-premises RBAC models must be adapted to support hybrid and multi-cloud environments, where users require access to multiple platforms and services. Organizations must implement federated identity management and single sign-on (SSO) solutions to ensure that RBAC policies are enforced consistently across all systems. Extending RBAC to third-party vendors and contractors is also critical, as external users often require temporary access to corporate resources. By implementing just-in-time (JIT) access provisioning and enforcing SOD policies for external users, organizations can mitigate the risks associated with third-party access.

Automation plays a key role in the successful enforcement of RBAC and SOD policies. Identity governance and administration (IGA) solutions provide automated role management, real-time policy enforcement, and continuous monitoring of access rights. AI-driven identity analytics can help organizations detect potential SOD violations by analyzing user behavior, identifying anomalies, and recommending corrective actions. By leveraging automation, organizations can reduce the administrative burden of managing RBAC while ensuring that SOD policies are consistently applied across all access control systems.

Despite its advantages, RBAC implementation can present challenges, particularly in large and complex organizations. Defining and managing a large number of roles can become difficult, leading to role explosion, where an excessive number of roles complicates administration. To address this challenge, organizations should adopt a role-mining approach, analyzing existing access patterns to define optimal role structures. Machine learning algorithms can assist in role mining by identifying common access groupings and recommending role assignments based on actual usage patterns. By refining role definitions and reducing redundancy, organizations can maintain a streamlined RBAC framework that supports SOD enforcement without unnecessary complexity.

RBAC remains a foundational model for enforcing SOD in IAM, providing a structured and scalable approach to access control. By assigning permissions based on roles rather than individuals, organizations can reduce security risks, improve compliance, and simplify access management. Effective implementation of RBAC requires careful role design, conflict analysis, access certification, automation, and continuous monitoring. As organizations embrace digital transformation, RBAC must evolve to accommodate cloud environments, remote workforces, and dynamic security threats. By integrating RBAC with modern IAM solutions, organizations can strengthen their SOD policies, enhance security, and maintain regulatory compliance across their entire IT ecosystem.

Attribute-Based Access Control (ABAC) and SOD

Attribute-Based Access Control (ABAC) is a dynamic and flexible access control model that defines user permissions based on attributes rather than static roles. Unlike Role-Based Access Control (RBAC), which assigns access rights based on predefined roles, ABAC evaluates contextual factors, user characteristics, and resource attributes to determine access permissions in real time. This approach allows organizations to enforce Segregation of Duties (SOD) with greater precision, reducing security risks and preventing conflicts of interest. By leveraging a policy-driven framework, ABAC ensures that access decisions are based on granular attributes such as job function, department, clearance level, device type, location, and time of access.

ABAC enhances SOD by allowing organizations to enforce access policies dynamically based on changing conditions. Traditional RBAC systems may struggle with complex access control scenarios where multiple variables influence authorization decisions. In contrast, ABAC allows security administrators to define policies that consider multiple attributes simultaneously, ensuring that access permissions remain aligned with security policies and regulatory requirements. For example, an organization can implement ABAC policies that prevent a financial officer from approving their own transactions by evaluating both the requestor's role and the context of the request. By integrating SOD principles into ABAC policies, organizations can enforce stricter controls over critical business processes and prevent unauthorized actions.

The core principle of ABAC is the use of attributes to define access rules. These attributes can be classified into four main categories: user attributes, resource attributes, environmental attributes, and action attributes. User attributes include identity-related factors such as job title, department, security clearance, and employment status. Resource attributes define characteristics of the data or system being accessed, such as classification level, ownership, or sensitivity. Environmental attributes consider external factors such as time of access, geographic location, network security posture, and device trust level. Action attributes define the type of operation being performed, such as read, write, delete, or approve. By combining these attributes, ABAC policies can enforce dynamic access controls that adapt to real-time security conditions.

One of the key advantages of ABAC in enforcing SOD is its ability to prevent access conflicts by evaluating multiple risk factors before granting permissions. In traditional access control models, users may accumulate excessive privileges over time due to role changes or improper access provisioning. ABAC eliminates this risk by continuously evaluating attributes to determine whether access should be granted or denied based on policy rules. For example, an IT administrator with privileged access may be allowed to configure network settings but prevented from approving security changes in production environments. By enforcing fine-grained controls, ABAC ensures that users do not perform conflicting duties that could lead to security breaches or fraud.

ABAC also provides greater flexibility in managing access control policies across hybrid and multi-cloud environments. Many organizations operate in complex IT ecosystems where users require access to multiple applications, cloud services, and on-premises systems. Traditional RBAC models often struggle to scale in these environments, as role assignments must be manually defined and updated for each system. ABAC, on the other hand, allows organizations to define centralized policies that automatically adapt to different contexts. By using attribute-based rules, organizations can enforce SOD policies consistently across diverse platforms, reducing administrative overhead and improving security posture.

To effectively implement ABAC for SOD enforcement, organizations must define clear policy rules that specify which attribute combinations are permissible and which should trigger access restrictions. These policies should be structured in a way that aligns with business processes, regulatory requirements, and risk management strategies. For example, an organization may define an ABAC policy that prevents an employee from both requesting and approving expense reimbursements within the same system. This policy could evaluate user attributes such as job role, department, and transaction history, ensuring that no individual can bypass financial controls. Similarly, an ABAC policy could restrict access to highly sensitive data based on contextual attributes such as device security status or geographic location.

Another key aspect of ABAC in SOD enforcement is policy administration and governance. Organizations must establish a centralized policy management framework that ensures ABAC rules are consistently applied across all systems. Policy management tools and IAM solutions that support ABAC provide interfaces for defining, testing, and deploying access control policies. These solutions often include policy enforcement points (PEPs) and policy decision points (PDPs) that evaluate attributes in real time to determine whether access requests comply with SOD policies. By integrating ABAC with IAM governance tools, organizations can automate policy enforcement and reduce the risk of access control violations.

Monitoring and auditing are essential components of an effective ABAC-based SOD strategy. Organizations must continuously track access events, analyze policy decisions, and detect anomalies that indicate potential security risks. Security Information and Event Management (SIEM) systems can integrate with ABAC solutions to provide real-time monitoring and threat detection. By analyzing user activity and access patterns, organizations can identify suspicious behavior, such as unauthorized privilege escalation or repeated access attempts to restricted resources. Automated audit logs help organizations maintain compliance with industry regulations and provide documentation for security assessments.

The implementation of ABAC requires careful planning and integration with existing IAM frameworks. Organizations must first conduct a comprehensive analysis of their business processes to identify areas where SOD policies need to be enforced. This involves mapping out potential conflicts, defining attribute-based policies, and ensuring that policy enforcement mechanisms are in place. Organizations must also integrate ABAC with authentication and authorization services to ensure seamless access control management. By adopting a phased implementation approach, organizations can gradually transition from legacy access control models to an ABAC-based framework without disrupting business operations.

ABAC's ability to enforce contextual and dynamic access controls makes it an ideal solution for organizations looking to strengthen their SOD policies. By leveraging attribute-driven access rules, organizations can ensure that users only have the necessary permissions to perform their duties while preventing unauthorized actions. ABAC's scalability, flexibility, and automation capabilities allow organizations to maintain compliance with regulatory requirements, improve security posture, and reduce administrative complexity. As identity and access management evolves, ABAC will play an increasingly vital role in enforcing SOD policies across modern IT environments, ensuring that access control decisions remain adaptive, risk-aware, and aligned with business objectives.

Policy-Based Access Control (PBAC) in SOD

Policy-Based Access Control (PBAC) is an advanced access management model that governs permissions based on predefined policies that take into account various factors such as user attributes, system context, and organizational rules. Unlike traditional access control models like Role-Based Access Control (RBAC), which assign permissions based on static roles, PBAC dynamically evaluates access requests against a set of policies to determine whether a user should be granted or denied access. This approach provides organizations with a highly flexible and scalable method for enforcing Segregation of Duties (SOD) by ensuring that access decisions are made in alignment with security policies, compliance requirements, and business objectives.

PBAC enhances SOD by allowing organizations to define granular access policies that explicitly prevent conflicts of interest and unauthorized actions. With PBAC, organizations can implement rules that dynamically restrict access based on contextual factors such as time of access, location, device security posture, and real-time risk assessments. This ensures that employees, contractors, and third-party users cannot bypass SOD policies by accumulating excessive privileges or assuming conflicting roles. The ability to enforce access decisions dynamically allows organizations to maintain stricter control over sensitive operations, reducing the risk of fraud, insider threats, and compliance violations.

One of the key principles of PBAC in SOD enforcement is the separation of policy definition and policy enforcement. In a PBAC framework, access control policies are centrally defined by security administrators and compliance teams, ensuring that they align with organizational risk management strategies. These policies are then enforced at multiple layers, including applications, databases, and identity management systems, ensuring consistency across the entire IT infrastructure. By centralizing policy management, organizations can reduce administrative overhead, eliminate inconsistencies, and simplify the process of enforcing SOD rules across different business functions.

A PBAC-driven SOD model is particularly effective in complex organizations where users require access to multiple systems and applications with varying levels of sensitivity. Traditional access control models often struggle with managing complex access scenarios, leading to situations where users inadvertently accumulate conflicting privileges. PBAC mitigates this risk by continuously evaluating access requests against predefined policies, ensuring that users only receive permissions that comply with SOD requirements. For example, in a financial institution, a PBAC policy can prevent an employee who initiates payments from also approving them, regardless of their assigned role. This ensures that financial transactions are subject to appropriate oversight, reducing the risk of fraudulent activities.

PBAC policies are designed using a rule-based approach that evaluates multiple attributes before granting access. These policies can include conditions such as job title, department, security clearance, time of day, and risk score. By incorporating risk-aware decision-making into access control policies, PBAC ensures that high-risk actions require additional approvals or justifications before being executed. This level of dynamic enforcement is crucial for maintaining SOD integrity in environments where business processes frequently change, and access requirements evolve over time.

One of the major advantages of PBAC in SOD enforcement is its ability to integrate with real-time monitoring and auditing systems. By continuously analyzing access logs, security teams can detect policy violations, investigate unauthorized activities, and refine policies to improve enforcement. PBAC solutions often integrate with Security Information and Event Management (SIEM) platforms, allowing organizations to detect anomalies and trigger automated responses when SOD conflicts occur. For instance, if an employee attempts to access both procurement and payment approval functions within an enterprise resource planning (ERP) system, PBAC can automatically block the request and generate an alert for security teams to review.

Automating SOD enforcement through PBAC reduces reliance on manual access reviews and minimizes the likelihood of human error. Organizations traditionally conduct periodic access certification campaigns to verify that employees do not have conflicting privileges, but these reviews can be time-consuming and ineffective when performed manually. PBAC eliminates the need for manual intervention by enforcing real-time policy evaluations that dynamically adjust user permissions based on current risk conditions. This not only improves security but also ensures continuous compliance with regulatory frameworks such as Sarbanes-Oxley (SOX), the General Data Protection Regulation (GDPR), and the Payment Card Industry Data Security Standard (PCI DSS).

Cloud adoption and the rise of hybrid IT environments have made SOD enforcement more challenging, as users require access across multiple cloud platforms, on-premises systems, and remote work environments. PBAC addresses these challenges by providing a unified access control model that can be applied across diverse infrastructure landscapes. Cloud Identity Providers (IdPs) and federated authentication systems can integrate with PBAC solutions to enforce SOD policies consistently across Software-as-a-Service (SaaS) applications, Infrastructure-as-a-Service (IaaS) platforms, and internal enterprise applications. By leveraging PBAC, organizations can ensure that SOD policies remain enforceable regardless of where users access corporate resources.

Implementing PBAC for SOD enforcement requires organizations to establish a comprehensive policy governance framework. This includes defining clear policy objectives, conducting risk assessments, and collaborating with business units to identify critical SOD requirements. Security and compliance teams must work together to design policies that accurately reflect business needs while minimizing security risks. Policies should be periodically reviewed and updated to adapt to changes in business processes, regulatory mandates, and emerging security threats. By continuously refining access control policies, organizations can maintain a proactive approach to enforcing SOD and mitigating access-related risks.

Organizations must also invest in training and awareness programs to ensure that employees and administrators understand PBAC-based SOD enforcement. Unlike traditional access control models, PBAC requires a shift in mindset, as access decisions are based on contextual policies rather than static role assignments. Employees must be educated on the importance of policy-based controls and how SOD policies impact their access to systems and data. Administrators must receive training on policy creation, policy enforcement mechanisms, and monitoring techniques to effectively manage PBAC solutions. A well-informed workforce helps ensure that SOD policies are not only technically enforced but also adhered to in daily business operations.

As organizations continue to embrace digital transformation, the need for adaptive, risk-aware access control models has become more critical than ever. PBAC provides a highly flexible and efficient framework for enforcing SOD policies, ensuring that users receive appropriate access based on real-time security conditions and business rules. By implementing PBAC, organizations can achieve greater visibility, automation, and control over access management while reducing the risk of fraud, compliance violations, and unauthorized activities. The ability to dynamically evaluate access requests and enforce granular policies makes PBAC an essential tool in modern IAM strategies, strengthening security postures and ensuring operational integrity across enterprise environments.

Access Control Models and Their Impact on SOD

Access control models play a fundamental role in enforcing security policies within an organization by determining how permissions are granted, managed, and enforced across various systems. These models define the mechanisms that restrict access to resources, ensuring that users only have the necessary permissions to perform their duties while preventing unauthorized actions. The choice of an access control model has a direct impact on the enforcement of Segregation of Duties (SOD), as it determines how conflicting roles and responsibilities are assigned and monitored. Organizations must carefully evaluate different access control models to ensure that they align with their SOD policies, regulatory requirements, and security objectives.

One of the most widely used access control models is Role-Based Access Control (RBAC), which assigns permissions based on predefined roles. In an RBAC system, users are grouped into roles that correspond to specific job functions, and each role is granted a set of permissions necessary to perform its duties. RBAC is highly effective in enforcing SOD because it allows organizations to define clear role hierarchies that prevent users from assuming conflicting duties. By structuring access rights based on job roles, RBAC ensures that employees cannot accumulate excessive privileges over time, reducing the risk of fraud and unauthorized transactions. However, RBAC can become complex in large organizations where role explosion occurs, requiring frequent role adjustments and access reviews to maintain compliance with SOD policies.

Another access control model that influences SOD enforcement is Attribute-Based Access Control (ABAC). Unlike RBAC, which relies on predefined roles, ABAC dynamically grants or denies access based on multiple attributes such as user identity, job title, department, location, time of access, and device security status. ABAC provides a more granular and flexible approach to access control, allowing organizations to define SOD policies based on real-time contextual information. This means that access decisions are not solely based on a user's assigned role but also take into account situational factors that may impact security and compliance. ABAC is particularly useful in environments where users frequently change roles or require temporary access to sensitive resources, as it ensures that permissions are dynamically adjusted based on current conditions.

Policy-Based Access Control (PBAC) is another access control model that significantly impacts SOD by enforcing access decisions through predefined security policies. PBAC defines rules that dictate how access is granted based on business policies, risk factors, and regulatory requirements. Organizations using PBAC can implement fine-grained SOD policies that automatically detect and prevent conflicts of interest before granting permissions. For example, a PBAC policy can restrict an employee from both submitting and approving purchase orders within an enterprise resource planning (ERP) system, ensuring that financial transactions are subject to proper oversight. PBAC's policy-driven approach enables organizations to enforce SOD dynamically, adapting to evolving business needs and compliance requirements without requiring manual intervention.

Discretionary Access Control (DAC) is another model that affects SOD enforcement but presents certain challenges in maintaining strict access segregation. In a DAC system, access rights are granted at the discretion of data owners, allowing them to decide who can access specific resources. While DAC offers flexibility, it also introduces security risks, as users with sufficient privileges may unintentionally or deliberately grant access to unauthorized individuals. This lack of centralized control makes it difficult to enforce SOD consistently, as data owners may inadvertently create conflicts by assigning overlapping permissions to employees. Organizations using DAC must implement additional oversight mechanisms, such as periodic access reviews and approval workflows, to ensure that SOD policies are not violated.

Mandatory Access Control (MAC), in contrast, provides a more structured and rigid approach to access control by enforcing strict security classifications and predefined rules. MAC is commonly used in government, military, and high-security environments where data classification levels dictate access privileges. In a MAC system, users are assigned security labels, and access to resources is determined based on predefined security policies rather than user discretion. This model is highly effective in enforcing SOD because access decisions are strictly controlled and cannot be overridden by individual users. However, the inflexibility of MAC can make it challenging to implement in dynamic business environments where users frequently require temporary access or cross-functional collaboration. Organizations that adopt MAC must carefully balance security with operational efficiency to ensure that SOD policies do not hinder business productivity.

The Zero Trust security model has gained prominence in recent years and has a significant impact on SOD enforcement. Unlike traditional access control models that rely on perimeter-based security, Zero Trust operates under the assumption that no user or device should be trusted by default. Instead, access is continuously verified based on identity authentication, device security posture, and real-time risk assessments. Zero Trust enforces SOD by implementing least privilege access, ensuring that users receive only the minimum permissions required for their tasks. This model integrates with IAM solutions, multi-factor authentication (MFA), and continuous monitoring tools to detect and prevent unauthorized access attempts. Zero Trust's real-time verification approach strengthens SOD enforcement by continuously evaluating whether users should retain access to sensitive systems and data.

Organizations must also consider the impact of access control models on cloud environments, where traditional SOD enforcement methods may not be sufficient. Cloud Identity and Access Management (Cloud IAM) solutions provide role-based, attribute-based, and policy-based access control mechanisms that extend SOD enforcement to cloud applications and services. In multi-cloud and hybrid IT environments, organizations must ensure that SOD policies are consistently applied across different platforms, preventing users from obtaining conflicting privileges across cloud and on-premises systems. Identity federation and single sign-on (SSO) solutions further enhance SOD enforcement by centralizing authentication and access controls, ensuring that users follow the same access policies regardless of where they log in.

To effectively implement SOD, organizations must carefully select the access control model that best aligns with their security and compliance requirements. While RBAC provides structured role management, ABAC and PBAC offer greater flexibility by dynamically adjusting permissions based on real-time conditions. MAC enforces strict security controls but may be too rigid for dynamic business environments, while DAC introduces challenges in maintaining centralized SOD enforcement. The Zero Trust model strengthens SOD through continuous access verification, reducing the risk of privilege escalation and insider threats. By integrating the right access control model with IAM solutions, automated policy enforcement, and real-time monitoring, organizations can effectively enforce SOD policies, mitigate security risks, and maintain compliance with industry regulations.

Identifying Critical Access Risks in Organizations

Organizations face numerous access risks that can lead to security breaches, data loss, fraud, and regulatory non-compliance. As digital transformation accelerates and businesses rely more on cloud environments, hybrid IT infrastructures, and third-party integrations, the complexity of managing access risks has increased significantly. Identifying and mitigating critical access risks is essential to maintaining a strong security posture and ensuring that Segregation of Duties (SOD) policies are effectively enforced. By understanding the key risks associated with user access, organizations can implement appropriate controls to prevent unauthorized actions and limit exposure to threats.

One of the most significant access risks in organizations is excessive privilege accumulation. Over time, employees may accumulate access rights that exceed what is necessary for their job functions. This phenomenon, known as role creep, occurs when users retain permissions from previous roles or gain additional privileges due to improper access reviews. Excessive privileges create security vulnerabilities, as individuals with broad access can perform unauthorized actions, whether intentional or accidental. Attackers who compromise an overprivileged account can exploit excessive permissions to access sensitive data, manipulate financial transactions, or disable security controls. Regular access reviews, automated privilege deprovisioning, and least privilege enforcement are essential strategies for mitigating this risk.

Another major access risk is inadequate enforcement of SOD policies. SOD is designed to prevent conflicts of interest by ensuring that no single individual has control over an entire business process. Without proper enforcement, employees may gain access to conflicting functions, such as initiating and approving payments, modifying financial records, or managing security settings without oversight. These conflicts create opportunities for fraud, insider threats, and compliance violations. Organizations must conduct regular SOD risk assessments to identify access conflicts and implement corrective actions. Automated policy enforcement within Identity and Access Management (IAM) systems helps detect and prevent SOD violations in real time.

Privileged access misuse is another critical risk that organizations must address. Administrative and superuser accounts have elevated permissions that allow them to modify system configurations, access sensitive data, and manage user accounts. If these privileges are misused or fall into the wrong hands, they can cause severe damage to an organization's security and operations. Insider threats, rogue administrators, or external attackers who gain access to privileged accounts can manipulate systems, delete critical data, or bypass security controls. Implementing Privileged Access Management (PAM) solutions, enforcing multi-factor authentication (MFA), and monitoring privileged activity are essential measures to mitigate this risk.

Weak authentication mechanisms increase the likelihood of unauthorized access and credential-based attacks. Many security breaches occur due to compromised credentials, often obtained through phishing attacks, brute force attempts, or credential stuffing. If organizations rely on weak passwords, single-factor authentication, or outdated authentication protocols, attackers can easily gain unauthorized access to corporate systems. Strengthening authentication mechanisms through MFA, biometric authentication, and passwordless authentication significantly reduces the risk of unauthorized access. Organizations should also enforce strict password policies, requiring employees to use strong, unique passwords and update them regularly.

Orphaned accounts present another significant access risk, especially in organizations with high employee turnover or complex IT environments. Orphaned accounts refer to accounts that remain active even after an employee leaves the organization, a contractor's engagement ends, or a project is completed. If these accounts are not deactivated or removed promptly, they can be exploited by malicious actors to gain unauthorized access. Organizations must implement automated user lifecycle management processes to ensure that accounts are promptly deactivated when no longer needed. Regular access certification campaigns help identify and eliminate orphaned accounts before they become security liabilities.

Shared accounts and credentials pose serious security risks by making it difficult to track individual user activity and enforce accountability. When multiple employees share the same login credentials for critical systems, organizations lose visibility into who performed specific actions, increasing the risk of fraud and policy violations. Shared accounts also create compliance challenges, as they do not align with best practices for access control and auditability. Organizations should eliminate shared accounts wherever possible and implement individual user credentials for all access points. When shared access is necessary, solutions such as just-in-time (JIT) access provisioning and session recording can enhance accountability and security.

Third-party access introduces another layer of risk, as external vendors, contractors, and service providers often require access to corporate systems. Organizations that grant excessive privileges to third-party users without proper oversight risk exposing sensitive data to unauthorized individuals. Vendor accounts that are not properly monitored or deprovisioned can become attack vectors for cybercriminals. Third-party risk management should include strict access governance, zero-trust principles, and continuous monitoring of vendor activity. Organizations must enforce the principle of least privilege, granting external users only the access they need for a limited period.

Inconsistent access review processes weaken an organization's ability to detect and mitigate access risks. Many organizations conduct access reviews infrequently or rely on manual processes that fail to identify unauthorized privileges effectively. Without regular audits and automated access review mechanisms, users may retain access to critical systems long after they no longer need it. IAM solutions with automated access certification workflows help organizations maintain visibility into user privileges, detect anomalies, and enforce timely remediation actions. Security teams must collaborate with business units to ensure that access reviews are thorough and aligned with security policies.

Shadow IT, where employees use unauthorized applications, cloud services, or personal devices for work-related tasks, introduces significant access risks. When users bypass official IT channels and create accounts on unapproved platforms, organizations lose control over data security and compliance. Shadow IT can lead to unauthorized data sharing, security misconfigurations, and increased exposure to cyber threats. Organizations must implement strict policies governing the use of external applications, enforce cloud access security controls, and educate employees on the risks associated with unapproved software. Visibility tools such as Cloud Access Security Brokers (CASB) help detect and manage shadow IT activities.

Access risks are further amplified by inadequate logging and monitoring of user activity. Without comprehensive logging and real-time monitoring, organizations struggle to detect security incidents and investigate suspicious behavior. Insufficient monitoring allows malicious actors to operate undetected, increasing the likelihood of data breaches, insider threats, and policy violations. Organizations must implement centralized logging solutions, integrate security analytics tools, and establish automated alerting mechanisms to identify and respond to access-related threats proactively. Behavioral analytics and machine learning-driven anomaly detection can help security teams recognize deviations from normal access patterns.

Data access risks extend beyond user permissions to include improper data handling practices, lack of encryption, and insufficient data classification. Organizations must ensure that sensitive data is protected from unauthorized access and exposure. Data Loss Prevention (DLP) solutions, encryption technologies, and strict access control policies help mitigate the risk of data leaks and breaches. Implementing data classification frameworks ensures that access to highly confidential information is restricted based on sensitivity levels. Organizations must regularly review and refine data protection strategies to prevent unauthorized access and ensure compliance with industry regulations.

Identifying and mitigating critical access risks is essential for strengthening security, preventing fraud, and maintaining compliance. Organizations must take a proactive approach by implementing access controls, enforcing SOD policies, and continuously monitoring user activity. By addressing risks such as excessive privileges, orphaned accounts, shared credentials, third-party access, weak authentication, and shadow IT, organizations can significantly reduce their exposure to access-related threats. Integrating advanced IAM solutions, automating access reviews, and leveraging security analytics ensures that access risks are effectively managed, protecting the organization from potential security breaches and operational disruptions.

SOD Considerations in Privileged Access Management (PAM)

Privileged Access Management (PAM) is a critical security discipline that focuses on controlling and securing access to highly sensitive systems and data. Privileged accounts, such as system administrators, database administrators, network engineers, and cloud service managers, have elevated access rights that allow them to make system-wide changes, configure security settings, and access sensitive data. If these privileges are not properly managed, they can pose a significant security risk to an organization. Segregation of Duties (SOD) plays an essential role in PAM by ensuring that no single individual has unchecked control over privileged functions, thereby reducing the risk of insider threats, accidental misconfigurations, and unauthorized system access.

A major challenge in privileged access management is ensuring that privileged users do not accumulate excessive control over multiple critical processes. SOD addresses this issue by separating responsibilities so that individuals cannot perform conflicting duties without oversight. For example, an IT administrator responsible for creating user accounts should not have the authority to approve or audit those accounts. Similarly, a security officer who configures firewall rules should not be the same person who reviews network security logs for anomalies. By enforcing these separations, organizations can prevent privilege abuse and establish accountability for privileged actions.

One of the most effective ways to implement SOD in PAM is through the principle of least privilege. This security best practice ensures that privileged users are granted only the access necessary to perform their job functions and nothing more. Over time, without proper controls, administrators and other privileged users may accumulate excessive permissions, increasing the risk of unauthorized actions. Enforcing least privilege helps organizations minimize the potential damage that could result from compromised credentials, insider threats, or human errors. Implementing just-in-time (JIT) privileged access further strengthens SOD by granting temporary elevated privileges only when needed and revoking them immediately after the task is completed.

The enforcement of SOD in PAM requires organizations to define strict policies governing privileged access. These policies should establish clear guidelines on how privileged accounts are provisioned, used, and audited. Organizations must ensure that privileged users are not assigned conflicting roles that could lead to security risks or compliance violations. Automated policy enforcement tools integrated within PAM solutions help organizations detect and prevent SOD violations in real time. By defining policy-based access restrictions, organizations can ensure that privileged users operate within predefined security parameters and cannot bypass established security controls.

A key component of SOD in PAM is the implementation of multi-factor authentication (MFA) for privileged access. Since privileged accounts provide access to critical systems, requiring multiple forms of authentication significantly reduces the risk of unauthorized access. Even if a privileged account's credentials are compromised, MFA adds an additional security layer that prevents attackers from easily gaining control. Organizations should enforce strong authentication mechanisms for all privileged sessions and integrate PAM solutions with MFA to ensure that access requests are properly verified before granting elevated privileges.

Another critical consideration for SOD in PAM is session monitoring and auditing. Privileged users must be continuously monitored to detect unauthorized or suspicious activities. PAM solutions provide session recording and real-time monitoring capabilities that allow security teams to track privileged activities across systems. If an administrator attempts to perform an unauthorized action, automated alerts can be triggered, and security personnel can intervene. Session recordings provide a valuable audit trail for forensic investigations and compliance reporting. By maintaining a detailed record of privileged activities, organizations can ensure accountability and detect policy violations more effectively.

To maintain strong SOD controls within PAM, organizations must implement role-based access control (RBAC) and attribute-based access control (ABAC) frameworks. RBAC ensures that privileged users are assigned specific roles with predefined permissions, preventing unauthorized privilege escalation. ABAC extends this capability by dynamically granting access based on contextual attributes such as time of access, device security posture, or location. By combining RBAC and ABAC within a PAM framework, organizations can enforce more granular access restrictions and ensure that privileged users do not gain excessive control over critical systems.

The use of privileged access request workflows further strengthens SOD enforcement in PAM. Organizations should require privileged users to submit access requests that are subject to managerial approval before gaining elevated permissions. Access request workflows introduce an additional layer of oversight, ensuring that privileged access is granted based on legitimate business needs and not through unchecked administrative control. Automated approval processes integrated into PAM solutions streamline this workflow, allowing managers and security teams to review, approve, or reject privileged access requests based on predefined criteria.

Privileged identity lifecycle management is another important aspect of SOD in PAM. Organizations must ensure that privileged accounts are regularly reviewed and deprovisioned when no longer needed. Dormant or orphaned privileged accounts present a significant security risk, as they can be exploited by attackers to gain unauthorized access. Automated lifecycle management processes should include periodic access reviews, privilege recertification, and immediate deactivation of privileged accounts when an employee changes roles or leaves the organization. Maintaining strict oversight of privileged identities ensures that only authorized personnel have access to sensitive systems.

In cloud environments, SOD enforcement in PAM becomes even more challenging due to the decentralized nature of cloud resources and the increasing use of automation tools such as Infrastructure-as-Code (IaC) and DevOps pipelines. Cloud platforms often provide highly privileged access to administrators, allowing them to create, modify, and delete virtual resources with minimal oversight. Organizations must implement cloud-specific PAM solutions that enforce SOD by restricting access to cloud management consoles, applying conditional access policies, and monitoring privileged activities in real time. Implementing identity federation and single sign-on (SSO) also helps ensure that SOD policies are consistently applied across hybrid and multi-cloud environments.

Third-party access to privileged accounts introduces additional risks that organizations must address when enforcing SOD in PAM. Vendors, contractors, and external partners often require temporary privileged access to corporate systems for maintenance, support, or integration purposes. Without proper controls, third-party users may gain excessive permissions that violate SOD policies. Organizations should implement vendor access management solutions that enforce just-in-time (JIT) privileged access, require MFA for third-party users, and monitor all privileged sessions. Temporary access should be automatically revoked once the required tasks are completed, ensuring that external users do not retain privileged access indefinitely.

Organizations must continuously assess and refine their SOD policies within PAM to adapt to evolving security threats and regulatory requirements. Regular audits, penetration testing, and risk assessments help identify weaknesses in privileged access controls and ensure that SOD policies remain effective. Security teams should collaborate with compliance officers and IT administrators to update access control frameworks, review privileged access logs, and implement corrective measures where necessary. By adopting a proactive approach to SOD enforcement within PAM, organizations can mitigate risks, prevent unauthorized access, and maintain a secure and compliant IT environment.

Implementing SOD in Enterprise Applications

Segregation of Duties (SOD) is a critical security and compliance measure that ensures no single individual has complete control over key business processes in enterprise applications. Implementing SOD effectively in enterprise applications is essential for preventing fraud, unauthorized access, data breaches, and compliance violations. Organizations rely on various enterprise applications such as Enterprise Resource Planning (ERP) systems, Customer Relationship Management (CRM) platforms, Human Resource Management Systems (HRMS), and financial software to manage critical operations. These applications store and process sensitive business data, making them prime targets for insider threats and external attacks. Without a well-defined SOD framework, users may gain excessive privileges, allowing them to perform conflicting tasks without oversight.

A key consideration when implementing SOD in enterprise applications is defining the access control model that aligns with business processes. Organizations must assess which business functions require strict separation of duties and identify potential conflicts. In ERP systems, for example, financial transactions must be segregated to prevent fraud and mismanagement. An employee responsible for creating vendor records should not have the ability to approve payments to those vendors. Similarly, in HRMS applications, a user with access to payroll data should not be allowed to modify employee records without additional approvals. Identifying these risks is the first step in establishing a strong SOD enforcement strategy.

Role-Based Access Control (RBAC) is one of the most commonly used models for enforcing SOD in enterprise applications. RBAC assigns permissions based on predefined roles, ensuring that users only have access to the resources necessary for their job functions. Organizations must create well-defined roles within their applications and ensure that conflicting roles cannot be assigned to the same user. For example, in financial applications, the role responsible for initiating purchase orders should not be allowed to approve them. To prevent privilege accumulation, organizations must regularly review role assignments and adjust access rights based on job changes, promotions, or departmental transfers.

Attribute-Based Access Control (ABAC) offers a more dynamic approach to implementing SOD in enterprise applications by evaluating multiple contextual factors before granting access. Unlike RBAC, which relies on static role assignments, ABAC determines access based on attributes such as user identity, department, location, device security status, and risk level. Organizations can define policies that prevent conflicting duties based on real-time conditions. For example, an ABAC policy in an ERP system could allow a financial officer to approve invoices only if they are not the same person who submitted them. By leveraging ABAC, organizations can enhance SOD enforcement while maintaining operational flexibility.

Enterprise applications must integrate automated SOD controls to detect and prevent access conflicts before they become security risks. Many ERP and financial management systems offer built-in SOD conflict detection tools that analyze user permissions and highlight potential violations. These tools help organizations proactively identify risks and remediate conflicting access rights. Automated access control solutions can generate alerts when users attempt to gain conflicting privileges, preventing policy violations in real time. Additionally, IAM platforms can integrate with enterprise applications to enforce access governance and ensure that SOD policies are consistently applied across all systems.

Access certification and periodic reviews are essential for maintaining SOD compliance in enterprise applications. Organizations must establish a formal process for reviewing user access rights to ensure that employees do not accumulate excessive privileges over time. Automated access review campaigns allow managers to verify whether assigned permissions align with job functions and remove any unnecessary access. These reviews should be conducted regularly to identify and eliminate SOD violations before they lead to security incidents. Enterprise applications that support automated recertification workflows can streamline this process, reducing the administrative burden of manual access reviews.

Privileged access management (PAM) plays a crucial role in enforcing SOD in enterprise applications by restricting high-risk administrative functions. Privileged accounts, such as database administrators, application administrators, and IT security personnel, often have broad access to critical systems. Without proper oversight, privileged users may bypass SOD controls and perform unauthorized actions. Organizations must implement PAM solutions that enforce just-in-time (JIT) privileged access, requiring users to request temporary elevated permissions for specific tasks. Session monitoring, activity logging, and real-time alerts further strengthen SOD enforcement by ensuring that all privileged actions are recorded and subject to review.

SOD enforcement must extend beyond internal employees to include third-party vendors, contractors, and external consultants who require access to enterprise applications. Third-party access introduces additional risks, as external users may not be fully aware of an organization's security policies and compliance requirements. Organizations should implement vendor access management solutions that enforce least privilege access for external users, limiting their permissions to only what is necessary for their tasks. Just-in-time access provisioning, time-based access expiration, and continuous monitoring help ensure that third-party users do not violate SOD policies while accessing enterprise applications.

Cloud-based enterprise applications introduce unique challenges for SOD enforcement, as users require access across multiple cloud platforms and Software-as-a-Service (SaaS) applications. Traditional on-premises access control models may not be sufficient for managing SOD in cloud environments. Organizations must implement cloud IAM solutions that provide centralized access control, ensuring that SOD policies are enforced consistently across all cloud applications. Multi-factor authentication (MFA), conditional access policies, and AI-driven anomaly detection can further enhance security by preventing unauthorized access attempts. By extending SOD policies to cloud environments, organizations can maintain security and compliance while enabling remote and hybrid workforces.

Compliance with industry regulations is another critical aspect of implementing SOD in enterprise applications. Regulations such as the Sarbanes-Oxley Act (SOX), the General Data Protection Regulation (GDPR), and the Payment Card Industry Data Security Standard (PCI DSS) mandate strict access controls to protect sensitive data and prevent fraud. Organizations must ensure that their enterprise applications support regulatory compliance by enforcing SOD policies through automated access controls, continuous monitoring, and audit trails. Compliance teams must work closely with IT and security departments to align SOD policies with regulatory requirements and conduct regular audits to demonstrate adherence.

User education and awareness are essential for the successful implementation of SOD in enterprise applications. Employees, managers, and IT administrators must understand the importance of SOD policies and their role in maintaining security and compliance. Organizations should conduct regular training sessions to educate users on access control best practices, the risks of SOD violations, and procedures for requesting and approving access changes. Security awareness programs help ensure that employees adhere to SOD policies and recognize the importance of preventing conflicts of interest in enterprise applications.

As organizations continue to adopt digital transformation initiatives, the need for effective SOD enforcement in enterprise applications becomes increasingly critical. By implementing RBAC and ABAC models, leveraging automated conflict detection tools, conducting regular access reviews, integrating PAM solutions, managing third-party access, securing cloud applications, and ensuring regulatory compliance, organizations can effectively enforce SOD policies while maintaining operational efficiency. Continuous monitoring, automation, and user awareness further strengthen SOD enforcement, ensuring that enterprise applications remain secure, compliant, and resilient against access-related risks.

The Role of IAM Tools in SOD Enforcement

Identity and Access Management (IAM) tools play a crucial role in enforcing Segregation of Duties (SOD) within organizations by providing mechanisms to manage, control, and monitor user access to critical systems and data. SOD enforcement is essential for reducing the risk of fraud, insider threats, unauthorized access, and compliance violations. Without robust IAM solutions, organizations may struggle to implement and maintain effective SOD policies, leading to security gaps and increased exposure to operational and financial risks. IAM tools provide a structured framework for access control, ensuring that users only have the permissions necessary for their job functions while preventing conflicts of interest.

One of the primary functions of IAM tools in SOD enforcement is user provisioning and deprovisioning. Properly managing user accounts and their associated permissions is essential for maintaining access control integrity. IAM solutions automate the process of onboarding new employees, granting them the appropriate access based on predefined roles and responsibilities. Similarly, when employees change roles, transfer departments, or leave the organization, IAM tools ensure that their access rights are updated or revoked accordingly. This prevents privilege accumulation, which can lead to excessive access rights that violate SOD policies. Automated provisioning also reduces the administrative burden on IT teams while maintaining consistency in access control enforcement.

Role-Based Access Control (RBAC) and Attribute-Based Access Control (ABAC) are key features of IAM tools that support SOD enforcement. RBAC assigns user permissions based on predefined roles, ensuring that individuals only have access to the systems and data necessary for their job functions. IAM tools help organizations design and enforce RBAC policies by mapping business roles to specific permissions, preventing users from being assigned conflicting roles. ABAC extends this capability by incorporating dynamic attributes such as job title, department, location, and security clearance into access control decisions. By leveraging ABAC, IAM solutions can enforce context-aware SOD policies, ensuring that access is granted based on real-time conditions rather than static role assignments.

IAM tools also play a vital role in enforcing least privilege access, a critical principle for maintaining SOD compliance. Least privilege access ensures that users have the minimum permissions required to perform their tasks and nothing more. IAM solutions continuously evaluate user access requests, ensuring that excessive permissions are not granted. By enforcing fine-grained access control, IAM tools prevent privilege escalation and reduce the risk of unauthorized activities. Automated access reviews and policy enforcement mechanisms further strengthen SOD compliance by identifying and remediating excessive access rights before they become security threats.

Access certification and periodic access reviews are essential components of SOD enforcement, and IAM tools provide automation for these processes. Organizations must regularly review user access rights to ensure compliance with SOD policies and regulatory requirements. IAM solutions facilitate automated access certification campaigns, allowing managers and compliance officers to review and validate user permissions. If access conflicts or SOD violations are detected, IAM tools provide workflows for corrective actions such as access revocation, reassignment, or escalation for further review. Automating access reviews reduces the risk of human error and ensures that organizations maintain continuous compliance with internal policies and external regulations.

Privileged Access Management (PAM) is another critical function within IAM solutions that directly impacts SOD enforcement. Privileged accounts, such as system administrators, database administrators, and security engineers, have elevated access rights that can bypass traditional access controls. If not properly managed, privileged users may accumulate excessive control over critical systems, violating SOD principles. IAM tools that include PAM capabilities ensure that privileged access is granted on a just-in-time (JIT) basis, requiring approval before elevated permissions are granted. Session monitoring, recording, and logging further enhance SOD compliance by providing visibility into privileged user activities, ensuring accountability, and detecting unauthorized actions.

IAM tools also support automated SOD conflict detection by analyzing user roles, permissions, and access patterns to identify potential violations. Advanced IAM solutions use artificial intelligence (AI) and machine learning (ML) to detect anomalies in user behavior and access privileges. AI-driven analytics can identify high-risk role combinations, flag suspicious access attempts, and recommend corrective actions to prevent policy violations. By leveraging data-driven insights, organizations can proactively enforce SOD policies and mitigate risks before they escalate into security incidents.

Integration with Security Information and Event Management (SIEM) systems enhances IAM tools' capabilities in SOD enforcement. SIEM platforms collect and analyze security event data from multiple sources, including IAM systems, firewalls, and application logs. By integrating IAM tools with SIEM solutions, organizations can correlate access control events with broader security threats, identifying patterns of unauthorized access, policy violations, or privilege abuse. Real-time alerts and automated incident response workflows ensure that security teams can quickly respond to SOD violations, minimizing potential damage and preventing fraudulent activities.

Cloud-based IAM solutions have become increasingly important in modern IT environments, where organizations operate across hybrid and multi-cloud infrastructures. Traditional on-premises IAM systems may not be sufficient for managing SOD compliance in cloud applications and services. Cloud Identity Providers (IdPs) and federated identity management solutions extend IAM controls to cloud platforms, ensuring that SOD policies are enforced consistently across all environments. IAM tools that support single sign-on (SSO), multi-factor authentication (MFA), and identity federation help secure cloud access while maintaining compliance with SOD policies. Automated provisioning and deprovisioning for cloud applications further reduce the risk of access misconfigurations and policy violations.

Third-party and vendor access management is another critical area where IAM tools help enforce SOD. Many organizations rely on external vendors, contractors, and business partners who require access to internal systems. Without proper access controls, third-party users may gain excessive privileges, increasing the risk of data breaches and compliance violations. IAM solutions provide secure vendor access management by enforcing just-in-time (JIT) access, time-restricted permissions, and continuous monitoring of third-party activities. By applying SOD principles to third-party access, organizations can reduce the risk of external security threats and maintain strict access governance.

IAM tools also support regulatory compliance by providing detailed audit logs, reporting capabilities, and policy enforcement mechanisms that align with industry standards. Regulations such as the Sarbanes-Oxley Act (SOX), the General Data Protection Regulation (GDPR), and the Health Insurance Portability and Accountability Act (HIPAA) require organizations to enforce strict access controls and SOD policies. IAM solutions generate compliance reports, track access policy adherence, and provide documentation for audit purposes. Automated reporting reduces the burden on compliance teams while ensuring that organizations remain in full compliance with regulatory requirements.

User training and awareness programs are enhanced through IAM tools by providing visibility into access requests, role assignments, and policy enforcement. Employees and managers must understand how SOD policies impact their access rights and business processes. IAM solutions can provide self-service access request portals, policy explanations, and security training resources that educate users on best practices for maintaining SOD compliance. By fostering a security-conscious culture, organizations can ensure that employees actively participate in access governance and adhere to SOD policies.

As organizations continue to face evolving cybersecurity threats and compliance challenges, the role of IAM tools in enforcing SOD becomes increasingly critical. By providing automated user provisioning, access certification, privileged access management, conflict detection, cloud integration, third-party access control, and compliance reporting, IAM solutions help organizations maintain security, reduce fraud risks, and prevent unauthorized access. The adoption of AI-driven analytics and automation further strengthens IAM tools' ability to enforce SOD dynamically, ensuring that access policies remain adaptive and responsive to emerging threats. Through continuous monitoring, policy refinement, and user awareness, organizations can leverage IAM solutions to build a secure, compliant, and well-governed access management framework.

Automating SOD Policy Enforcement

Segregation of Duties (SOD) is a fundamental principle in Identity and Access Management (IAM) that ensures no single individual has complete control over critical business processes. By enforcing SOD policies, organizations can prevent fraud, insider threats, and operational risks while ensuring compliance with regulatory frameworks. However, manual enforcement of SOD policies is inefficient, error-prone, and difficult to scale, especially in large enterprises with complex access control requirements. Automating SOD policy enforcement allows organizations to streamline access management, reduce administrative overhead, and improve security by ensuring that conflicting access rights are continuously monitored and remediated in real time.

One of the key components of automating SOD policy enforcement is the implementation of identity governance and administration (IGA) solutions. IGA platforms provide centralized access control, allowing organizations to define, enforce, and monitor SOD policies across all systems and applications. These solutions integrate with IAM tools to automate user provisioning, access reviews, and policy enforcement, ensuring that users only have access to the resources required for their job functions. By leveraging automated workflows, organizations can eliminate manual intervention in access management processes, reducing the likelihood of human error and policy violations.

Automated role management is a crucial aspect of SOD policy enforcement. Many organizations rely on Role-Based Access Control (RBAC) to define user permissions based on job functions. Over time, role structures can become complex, leading to role creep and excessive privilege accumulation. Automated role mining tools analyze existing access patterns to identify optimal role structures and detect overlapping permissions that may violate SOD policies. These tools help organizations maintain clean and efficient role hierarchies, ensuring that users are assigned appropriate access levels without the risk of conflicting duties.

Real-time access conflict detection is another critical capability of automated SOD enforcement. Traditional access reviews often occur periodically, leaving gaps where SOD violations can go undetected. Automated solutions continuously monitor access rights and detect potential conflicts as soon as they arise. By integrating with enterprise applications, cloud services, and privileged access management (PAM) tools, these solutions analyze user permissions in real time and generate alerts when an SOD policy violation is detected. Organizations can then take immediate corrective actions, such as revoking conflicting permissions, reassigning roles, or requiring additional approvals before granting access.

Artificial intelligence (AI) and machine learning (ML) enhance automated SOD policy enforcement by providing advanced analytics and predictive risk assessment. AI-driven identity analytics can assess user behavior, identify anomalous access requests, and predict potential SOD violations before they occur. Machine learning models analyze historical access data to detect patterns that may indicate fraudulent activity or policy breaches. These insights enable organizations to proactively enforce SOD policies, reducing the risk of security incidents while improving overall access governance.

Automating access request and approval workflows strengthens SOD enforcement by ensuring that conflicting permissions are identified before access is granted. Traditional manual approval processes can be slow and ineffective, leading to delays in access provisioning or oversight gaps. Automated workflows streamline the approval process by integrating policy-based decision-making mechanisms. When a user requests access to a system, the IAM solution automatically evaluates whether the request violates any SOD policies. If a conflict is detected, the request is either denied or escalated for additional review. Automated approval workflows also enforce multi-level approvals for high-risk access requests, ensuring that sensitive permissions are reviewed by multiple stakeholders before being granted.

Privileged access management (PAM) solutions play a crucial role in automating SOD enforcement by securing high-risk administrative accounts. Privileged users often have elevated permissions that could allow them to bypass security controls or execute unauthorized transactions. Without proper oversight, privileged users can inadvertently violate SOD policies by assuming multiple conflicting responsibilities. PAM solutions enforce just-in-time (JIT) access provisioning, ensuring that privileged users receive elevated permissions only when necessary and only for a limited duration. Additionally, session monitoring and recording capabilities provide visibility into privileged activities, allowing security teams to detect and respond to policy violations in real time.

Automated access reviews and certification campaigns are essential for maintaining continuous SOD compliance. Many organizations struggle with periodic access reviews due to the complexity of manually evaluating user permissions across multiple systems. Automated access review solutions streamline this process by generating reports that highlight potential SOD conflicts and excessive privileges. Managers and compliance teams can review and certify user access rights through an intuitive interface, approving or revoking permissions as needed. By automating access reviews, organizations can ensure that SOD policies remain effective and that access rights are regularly validated without relying on time-consuming manual audits.

Cloud-based IAM solutions further enhance automated SOD policy enforcement by providing centralized access management across hybrid and multi-cloud environments. As organizations migrate to cloud services, maintaining consistent SOD policies across different platforms becomes challenging. Cloud Identity Providers (IdPs) integrate with IAM solutions to enforce SOD policies consistently, regardless of whether users access resources from on-premises systems, SaaS applications, or cloud infrastructure. Cloud-native IAM solutions also provide real-time visibility into access rights, allowing security teams to detect and remediate SOD violations across distributed environments.

Automating SOD enforcement also improves regulatory compliance by providing detailed audit trails and compliance reports. Regulations such as the Sarbanes-Oxley Act (SOX), General Data Protection Regulation (GDPR), and Payment Card Industry Data Security Standard (PCI DSS) require organizations to maintain strict access controls and prevent unauthorized transactions. Automated IAM solutions generate comprehensive logs that document access changes, policy violations, and remediation actions. Compliance teams can use these reports to demonstrate adherence to regulatory requirements during audits, reducing the risk of fines and penalties.

Organizations must also ensure that automated SOD enforcement aligns with business needs without creating operational bottlenecks. Overly restrictive SOD policies can hinder productivity by preventing employees from accessing necessary resources. Automated IAM solutions offer policy customization features that allow organizations to define risk-based SOD policies that balance security with operational efficiency. Risk scoring models help prioritize policy enforcement based on the sensitivity of access requests, ensuring that high-risk transactions receive stricter scrutiny while low-risk requests are processed with minimal disruption.

To maximize the benefits of automated SOD enforcement, organizations must invest in training and awareness programs. Employees, managers, and IT administrators must understand how automated SOD policies function and how access control decisions impact their workflows. Security awareness training ensures that users comply with access policies, recognize potential conflicts, and follow best practices for requesting and approving access. IAM solutions can provide self-service portals that allow users to view their current permissions, submit access requests, and understand why certain requests may be denied due to SOD restrictions.

By integrating automation into SOD policy enforcement, organizations can achieve greater efficiency, accuracy, and security in access management. Automated IAM solutions, AI-driven analytics, real-time monitoring, privileged access controls, and cloud-based access governance all contribute to a comprehensive SOD enforcement strategy. As security threats evolve and regulatory requirements become more stringent, organizations must continuously refine and improve their automated SOD enforcement mechanisms to maintain compliance, reduce risk, and ensure that access policies remain effective across their entire IT ecosystem.

Identity Governance and SOD

Identity governance is a critical component of modern cybersecurity and compliance strategies, ensuring that user access to enterprise systems is properly managed, monitored, and audited. It provides organizations with the ability to control who has access to what resources, how that access is granted, and whether it aligns with security policies and regulatory requirements. One of the most significant aspects of identity governance is enforcing Segregation of Duties (SOD), a fundamental principle that prevents conflicts of interest, insider threats, and fraud by ensuring that no single individual has excessive control over critical business processes. By integrating SOD into identity governance frameworks, organizations can strengthen security, improve accountability, and maintain compliance with industry regulations.

Identity governance solutions help organizations enforce SOD by defining access policies, automating provisioning and deprovisioning, and continuously monitoring user activities. Without a structured governance model, employees, contractors, and third-party users may accumulate unnecessary or conflicting privileges, increasing the risk of unauthorized transactions or security breaches. By implementing an identity governance framework, organizations can systematically assess access risks, detect SOD violations, and enforce corrective actions before they lead to compliance failures or financial losses.

A well-defined identity governance program begins with the establishment of policies that dictate how access is granted, reviewed, and revoked. These policies should outline the roles and responsibilities of employees and specify which duties must be segregated to prevent conflicts of interest. For example, in financial systems, identity governance policies should ensure that an employee responsible for initiating payments does not have the authority to approve them. Similarly, in IT environments, a system administrator who manages user accounts should not be able to approve access requests without oversight. By defining clear policies, organizations can establish a foundation for enforcing SOD consistently across all applications and systems.

Role-Based Access Control (RBAC) and Attribute-Based Access Control (ABAC) play a significant role in identity governance and SOD enforcement. RBAC structures access rights based on predefined roles, ensuring that employees receive only the permissions necessary for their job functions. Identity governance solutions integrate RBAC models to prevent conflicting role assignments that could violate SOD policies. ABAC, on the other hand, allows organizations to enforce more dynamic access controls by evaluating contextual attributes such as job title, department, location, or device security posture. By leveraging ABAC within identity governance frameworks, organizations can enforce SOD dynamically and prevent access conflicts in real time.

Identity lifecycle management is another crucial aspect of identity governance that directly impacts SOD enforcement. Organizations must ensure that user access is properly managed throughout the entire employment lifecycle, from onboarding to role changes to offboarding. Without automated identity lifecycle management, employees may retain access to systems they no longer need, leading to role creep and potential SOD violations. Identity governance solutions automate the provisioning and deprovisioning of user accounts, ensuring that access rights are updated in response to job changes or employment termination. By enforcing lifecycle-based access management, organizations can reduce the risk of unauthorized access and maintain compliance with SOD policies.

Automated access certification campaigns play a key role in identity governance and SOD enforcement by ensuring that user access rights are reviewed and validated regularly. Organizations must conduct periodic access reviews to verify that employees have only the necessary permissions required for their job functions. Identity governance solutions automate these reviews by generating reports that highlight SOD conflicts, excessive privileges, and unauthorized access. Security and compliance teams can then approve, modify, or revoke access based on the review findings. Automating access certification not only reduces administrative overhead but also ensures that SOD policies are consistently enforced and documented for audit purposes.

Privileged access management (PAM) is another essential component of identity governance that strengthens SOD enforcement. Privileged users, such as system administrators and database managers, have elevated permissions that allow them to perform critical operations. Without proper governance, privileged users may bypass SOD policies, leading to security risks and compliance violations. Identity governance solutions integrate with PAM tools to enforce just-in-time (JIT) privileged access, requiring approvals before elevated permissions are granted. Session monitoring, recording, and logging further enhance governance by providing visibility into privileged activities and ensuring accountability. By integrating PAM with identity governance, organizations can effectively manage privileged access while enforcing SOD policies.

Identity governance solutions also support real-time monitoring and anomaly detection, helping organizations identify potential SOD violations before they become security incidents. Advanced analytics powered by artificial intelligence (AI) and machine learning (ML) can detect unusual access patterns, privilege escalations, or attempts to bypass access controls. For example, if an employee suddenly gains access to conflicting roles within an ERP system, identity governance tools can trigger alerts, block the access request, or require additional approvals. AI-driven identity governance enables proactive enforcement of SOD policies, reducing the likelihood of fraud and unauthorized access.

Integration with regulatory compliance frameworks is a key benefit of identity governance in SOD enforcement. Organizations must comply with various regulations, such as the Sarbanes-Oxley Act (SOX), the General Data Protection Regulation (GDPR), and the Health Insurance Portability and Accountability Act (HIPAA), all of which mandate strict access control measures. Identity governance solutions provide detailed audit logs, compliance reports, and policy enforcement mechanisms to help organizations meet these regulatory requirements. Automated reporting capabilities streamline compliance audits by providing visibility into user access, policy violations, and remediation actions. By aligning identity governance with regulatory mandates, organizations can reduce compliance risks and avoid costly penalties.

Identity governance also extends to third-party and vendor access management, an area where SOD enforcement is particularly challenging. External contractors, consultants, and business partners often require access to internal systems, increasing the risk of unauthorized activities. Without proper governance, third-party users may receive excessive privileges that violate SOD policies. Identity governance solutions enforce least privilege access for external users by granting time-restricted, just-in-time access and continuously monitoring their activities. Vendor risk assessments and automated access reviews further strengthen governance, ensuring that third-party access remains compliant with SOD policies.

User training and awareness programs complement identity governance by educating employees on the importance of SOD policies and access management best practices. Identity governance solutions can integrate with self-service access request portals, providing users with clear visibility into their current permissions and policy restrictions. By increasing awareness of SOD policies, organizations can foster a security-conscious culture where employees actively participate in maintaining access governance and compliance. Security awareness training helps prevent accidental policy violations and ensures that users follow proper procedures when requesting, approving, or modifying access rights.

Organizations must continuously refine and optimize their identity governance strategies to adapt to evolving security threats and regulatory requirements. Regular audits, policy updates, and risk assessments help ensure that SOD policies remain effective and aligned with business needs. Identity governance solutions provide the automation, visibility, and policy enforcement mechanisms necessary to maintain strong SOD controls across all systems and applications. By integrating IAM, PAM, and advanced analytics into their identity governance frameworks, organizations can enhance security, reduce operational risks, and maintain compliance with industry standards.

SOD Policy Definition and Documentation

Segregation of Duties (SOD) is a fundamental principle in risk management and security, ensuring that no single individual has complete control over critical business functions. Defining and documenting an effective SOD policy is essential for organizations to prevent fraud, insider threats, and regulatory violations while maintaining operational integrity. A well-structured SOD policy provides clear guidelines on how access to systems, data, and processes should be distributed among employees, ensuring that conflicting responsibilities are assigned to separate individuals. Proper documentation of these policies ensures consistency, compliance, and accountability, allowing organizations to enforce SOD controls effectively across various departments and business processes.

The process of defining an SOD policy begins with identifying critical business functions and the associated risks. Organizations must analyze their operations to determine which activities require strict separation of duties to mitigate financial fraud, data manipulation, and security breaches. Common areas that require SOD enforcement include financial transactions, procurement approvals, payroll processing, IT administration, and regulatory compliance functions. For example, in an accounting system, an employee responsible for recording transactions should not be allowed to approve payments. Similarly, in IT security, an administrator who manages user accounts should not have the ability to approve access requests without oversight. By identifying these critical functions, organizations can establish the foundation for SOD enforcement.

Once key business functions have been identified, organizations must define SOD policies that clearly outline access restrictions and control mechanisms. These policies should specify which roles and responsibilities must be segregated to prevent conflicts of interest. An effective SOD policy should include detailed rules that dictate which combinations of access privileges are prohibited and how exceptions should be handled. For example, a policy might state that employees in the finance department cannot have access to both accounts payable and accounts receivable systems simultaneously. IT administrators should not have access to modify audit logs, ensuring that no single individual can tamper with security records. By documenting these rules, organizations can create a structured framework for enforcing SOD policies consistently.

Roles and responsibilities must be clearly defined within the SOD policy to ensure proper enforcement. Organizations should categorize job functions based on access needs and potential conflicts, assigning each function to a specific role. Role-Based Access Control (RBAC) and Attribute-Based Access Control (ABAC) models can be used to structure access permissions in alignment with SOD requirements. RBAC assigns users to predefined roles with associated permissions, ensuring that conflicting duties are not assigned to the same individual. ABAC takes a more dynamic approach by incorporating contextual attributes such as department, job level, and location to determine access rights. By defining roles with clear boundaries, organizations can prevent unauthorized privilege accumulation and reduce security risks.

An effective SOD policy should also establish approval workflows and access request procedures to ensure proper oversight. Employees requesting access to critical systems or functions must go through a structured approval process that involves multiple levels of review. Access requests should be evaluated based on predefined criteria to ensure they do not violate SOD rules. Automated workflows integrated into Identity and Access Management (IAM) systems help streamline these processes by enforcing approval hierarchies and detecting potential conflicts in real time. Access requests that pose an SOD violation should be escalated to higher management or compliance officers for further review before approval.

Exception management is an important component of SOD policy definition and documentation. There may be instances where temporary access to conflicting functions is necessary due to business needs, emergencies, or employee absences. SOD policies should define a structured process for managing exceptions, ensuring that they are approved by appropriate authorities and monitored closely.

Organizations should require additional compensating controls for approved exceptions, such as dual approvals, session monitoring, or increased audit logging. Documentation of exceptions should include justification for the access request, approval records, and expiration dates to ensure that temporary access is revoked when no longer needed.

Regular access reviews and audits must be incorporated into SOD policy documentation to maintain ongoing compliance. Organizations should conduct periodic assessments of user access rights to verify that employees do not have conflicting privileges. Automated access review tools help identify SOD violations by analyzing access patterns and role assignments across enterprise systems. Managers and compliance teams should review these reports and take corrective actions where necessary. Access certifications should be conducted at regular intervals, ensuring that access rights remain aligned with job responsibilities and security policies. By documenting access review procedures, organizations can demonstrate compliance with regulatory requirements and maintain accountability.

Training and awareness programs should be included in SOD policy documentation to ensure that employees understand the importance of segregation of duties. Employees, managers, and IT administrators must be educated on SOD principles, access request procedures, and policy enforcement mechanisms. Security awareness training helps employees recognize potential conflicts of interest and understand how their roles impact organizational security. Providing employees with clear guidelines on SOD compliance reduces the likelihood of accidental policy violations and ensures that access control measures are followed consistently.

SOD policy documentation should also address integration with regulatory compliance frameworks. Many industries are subject to strict regulations that mandate the enforcement of access controls and SOD policies. Regulations such as the Sarbanes-Oxley Act (SOX), the General Data Protection Regulation (GDPR), and the Payment Card Industry Data Security Standard (PCI DSS) require organizations to implement controls that prevent unauthorized access and financial fraud. SOD policy documents should outline how access controls align with these regulations, ensuring that organizations remain in compliance. Automated reporting and audit logs should be maintained to provide evidence of policy enforcement during regulatory audits.

Technology plays a crucial role in SOD policy enforcement, and documentation should specify how IAM solutions, Privileged Access Management (PAM) tools, and security monitoring systems support policy implementation. IAM solutions help enforce SOD by automating access control, detecting policy violations, and providing real-time alerts. PAM tools ensure that privileged accounts are managed securely, preventing administrators from bypassing SOD controls. Security monitoring solutions integrate with IAM platforms to track user activity and detect anomalies that may indicate an SOD violation. By documenting how these technologies are utilized, organizations can establish a comprehensive approach to SOD enforcement.

As business environments evolve, SOD policies must be regularly reviewed and updated to reflect organizational changes, emerging threats, and new compliance requirements. Policy documentation should include guidelines for policy updates, version control, and periodic assessments. Organizations should designate responsible personnel to oversee policy revisions and ensure that any changes are communicated effectively across all departments. Keeping SOD policies up to date ensures that they remain relevant and effective in preventing security risks.

By defining and documenting SOD policies in a structured manner, organizations can establish a strong foundation for access control, regulatory compliance, and risk management. Clearly articulated policies provide consistency in enforcement, ensuring that SOD principles are applied uniformly across all business functions. Proper documentation enhances accountability, streamlines audits, and supports automated enforcement mechanisms, ultimately strengthening the organization's overall security posture.

Business Process Mapping for SOD

Business process mapping is a critical step in implementing Segregation of Duties (SOD) within an organization. It provides a structured approach to identifying, analyzing, and documenting key business processes to ensure that access controls align with security and compliance requirements. Without proper mapping, organizations may struggle to enforce SOD policies effectively, increasing the risk of fraud, unauthorized transactions, and operational inefficiencies. By mapping business processes, organizations gain a clear understanding of how tasks flow across different departments, who is responsible for each step, and where potential conflicts of interest or access risks may arise.

The process of business mapping begins with identifying critical business functions that require SOD enforcement. These functions often include financial transactions, procurement, payroll processing, IT administration, compliance reporting, and other operational activities that involve sensitive data or high-risk transactions. Each function must be broken down into its individual steps, with clear documentation of roles and responsibilities assigned to employees. For example, in the accounts payable process, one employee may be responsible for submitting invoices, another for approving payments, and a separate individual for reconciling financial records. By mapping these responsibilities, organizations can ensure that no single individual has complete control over financial transactions, reducing the risk of fraud or errors.

Once critical functions have been identified, organizations must define key process flows that illustrate how information, approvals, and decisions move through the organization. Process mapping tools such as flowcharts, swimlane diagrams, and data flow models help visualize these workflows, making it easier to identify SOD conflicts. A well-structured process map should clearly outline who performs each step in the workflow, what actions they are authorized to take, and what controls are in place to prevent unauthorized activities. These visual representations help stakeholders understand potential weaknesses in access control policies and where SOD enforcement needs to be strengthened.

A key aspect of business process mapping for SOD is identifying role conflicts that may lead to policy violations. Organizations must analyze whether employees have overlapping access rights that could compromise security. Role conflict analysis involves cross-referencing job functions, user permissions, and approval workflows to detect potential conflicts. For instance, an employee with access to both vendor creation and payment processing in an ERP system creates a high-risk scenario where fraudulent transactions could occur. By systematically analyzing process maps, organizations can restructure role assignments, implement compensating controls, or introduce additional approval layers to mitigate risks.

Automation plays a significant role in streamlining business process mapping for SOD. Modern Identity and Access Management (IAM) solutions provide tools that automatically assess business processes, identify role conflicts, and enforce access controls. Automated policy enforcement ensures that employees are granted only the necessary permissions required for their job functions while preventing unauthorized access to conflicting duties. These solutions integrate with enterprise applications to continuously monitor process flows, detect access anomalies, and alert security teams when an SOD violation is detected. By leveraging automation, organizations can improve the accuracy and efficiency of SOD enforcement across complex business environments.

Business process mapping also helps organizations establish accountability by defining approval hierarchies and oversight mechanisms. Many business processes involve multiple layers of approvals, requiring proper documentation of who is responsible for reviewing and authorizing transactions. Clearly defined approval workflows ensure that decisions are reviewed by appropriate stakeholders before being executed. For example, in a procurement process, a manager may approve purchase requisitions, while a finance officer authorizes payment disbursements. Implementing workflow automation ensures that approvals follow established hierarchies and that unauthorized changes cannot be made without detection.

Risk assessment is another important component of business process mapping for SOD. Organizations must evaluate the level of risk associated with each process and determine which activities require the highest level of control. High-risk processes, such as financial reporting, data access management, and privileged account administration, require stricter SOD enforcement. Organizations can classify risks based on impact, likelihood, and potential financial or regulatory consequences. This assessment helps prioritize SOD controls, ensuring that the most critical processes receive the highest level of oversight. By mapping business processes and incorporating risk assessments, organizations can allocate resources effectively to mitigate the most significant threats.

Continuous monitoring and auditing of business processes ensure that SOD controls remain effective over time. Organizations must regularly review and update process maps to reflect changes in business operations, regulatory requirements, and security threats. Periodic audits help identify new access conflicts, detect unauthorized activities, and ensure compliance with SOD policies. Audit logs, access review reports, and exception handling records provide valuable insights into process efficiency and policy adherence. By maintaining up-to-date process maps, organizations can adapt to evolving risks and maintain a strong security posture.

Cloud adoption and digital transformation initiatives have introduced new challenges in business process mapping for SOD. As organizations migrate to cloud-based applications and hybrid IT environments, traditional access control models may not be sufficient to enforce SOD across distributed systems. Cloud identity governance solutions provide centralized visibility into user access, enabling organizations to apply consistent SOD policies across multiple platforms. Business process mapping in cloud environments requires integration with cloud-native IAM tools, multi-factor authentication (MFA), and real-time monitoring to ensure that SOD policies remain enforceable in dynamic infrastructures.

Organizations must also ensure that third-party access is accounted for in business process mapping for SOD. Vendors, contractors, and external partners often require access to internal systems, creating potential security risks if access is not properly managed. Business process maps should document how third-party access is granted, what controls are in place to limit privileges, and how vendor activities are monitored. Implementing least privilege access for external users, requiring time-bound access approvals, and continuously monitoring third-party interactions help reduce security risks associated with external access. By including third-party access in process mapping, organizations can prevent unauthorized activities and maintain compliance with security policies.

Training and awareness programs are essential for ensuring that employees understand the role of SOD in business processes. Organizations should provide training sessions that explain how process mapping supports SOD enforcement, the importance of adhering to access control policies, and the risks associated with policy violations. Employees should be encouraged to report potential SOD conflicts and seek guidance when unclear about role assignments. By fostering a culture of security awareness, organizations can strengthen adherence to SOD policies and reduce the likelihood of intentional or accidental access control violations.

As business environments continue to evolve, organizations must adopt a proactive approach to business process mapping for SOD. By continuously analyzing workflows, leveraging automation, integrating risk assessments, and maintaining clear documentation, organizations can enhance their ability to enforce SOD policies effectively. A well-defined business process map serves as a foundation for strong access control, regulatory compliance, and risk mitigation, ensuring that SOD enforcement remains a central component of security and governance frameworks.

SOD Risk Assessments and Audits

Segregation of Duties (SOD) is a fundamental principle in risk management and access control that ensures critical business processes are not executed by a single individual without oversight. The effectiveness of SOD policies relies heavily on continuous risk assessments and audits, which help organizations identify vulnerabilities, detect policy violations, and maintain compliance with security and regulatory requirements. Conducting regular SOD risk assessments and audits enables organizations to proactively mitigate fraud, insider threats, and operational risks by ensuring that users do not accumulate excessive or conflicting privileges. Without a structured approach to risk assessments and audits, organizations may struggle to enforce SOD policies effectively, increasing their exposure to security breaches and financial mismanagement.

The first step in conducting an SOD risk assessment is identifying high-risk business processes that require strict access control measures. Organizations must evaluate critical functions such as financial transactions, procurement, payroll processing, regulatory reporting, and IT administration to determine where access segregation is necessary. Each function should be analyzed to identify potential conflicts of interest, where a single user might have the ability to initiate, approve, and execute transactions without independent oversight. For example, in financial systems, an employee with both payment initiation and approval privileges presents a significant fraud risk. Similarly, in IT environments, a system administrator who manages user accounts and security logs can potentially manipulate audit records to conceal unauthorized actions. By identifying these high-risk scenarios, organizations can prioritize SOD enforcement efforts and allocate resources effectively.

Once high-risk areas have been identified, organizations must assess existing access controls to determine whether SOD policies are being enforced consistently. This involves reviewing user roles, permissions, and access assignments to detect any conflicts that may pose a security threat. Automated identity governance solutions play a crucial role in simplifying this process by analyzing user access rights across multiple systems and highlighting potential SOD violations. These solutions compare existing access configurations with predefined SOD policies to identify users who have accumulated conflicting privileges over time. Organizations can then take corrective actions such as revoking excessive permissions, restructuring role assignments, or implementing additional approval layers to strengthen access controls.

Risk assessments should also consider the impact and likelihood of SOD violations occurring within different business functions. Not all access conflicts pose the same level of risk, so organizations must prioritize their remediation efforts based on the potential consequences of policy violations. Risk scoring models help organizations quantify the severity of SOD conflicts by evaluating factors such as financial exposure, regulatory implications, data sensitivity, and the frequency of access. For instance, an access conflict that could result in unauthorized financial transactions may be classified as a high-risk issue requiring immediate remediation, whereas a lower-risk conflict, such as overlapping permissions in a non-critical system, may be addressed through periodic reviews. By classifying SOD risks based on impact and likelihood, organizations can develop a structured approach to risk mitigation.

In addition to risk assessments, conducting regular SOD audits is essential for verifying policy compliance and identifying gaps in access control enforcement. SOD audits involve systematically reviewing user activity, access changes, and policy violations to ensure that segregation principles are being maintained. Internal audit teams, compliance officers, and security personnel must work together to assess whether users are adhering to established SOD policies and whether any unauthorized actions have been performed. Audit reports provide valuable insights into the effectiveness of existing controls, helping organizations refine their policies and address any weaknesses in their access management frameworks.

A comprehensive SOD audit should include detailed access reviews that assess the appropriateness of user permissions. Organizations must examine whether employees, contractors, and third-party vendors have only the necessary access required for their job functions. These reviews should be conducted periodically to prevent role creep, where users accumulate excessive privileges over time due to changes in responsibilities or improper access provisioning. Automated access review solutions streamline this process by generating reports that highlight role conflicts, excessive permissions, and policy violations. Auditors can then validate these reports and take corrective actions to revoke or adjust access rights where necessary.

Audit logs and activity monitoring play a crucial role in SOD enforcement by providing visibility into user actions and system modifications. Organizations must maintain detailed logs of all access requests, privilege escalations, and transaction approvals to track compliance with SOD policies. Security Information and Event Management (SIEM) solutions integrate with IAM systems to analyze access patterns and detect suspicious activities that may indicate unauthorized actions. For example, if a user attempts to bypass approval workflows or escalates their own privileges without authorization, automated alerts can be triggered to notify security teams. Maintaining a comprehensive audit trail ensures accountability and allows organizations to investigate policy violations effectively.

External audits are also a key aspect of SOD compliance, particularly for organizations subject to regulatory requirements such as the Sarbanes-Oxley Act (SOX), the General Data Protection Regulation (GDPR), and the Payment Card Industry Data Security Standard (PCI DSS). Regulatory auditors assess whether organizations have implemented adequate SOD controls to prevent financial fraud, data breaches, and non-compliance penalties. Preparing for external audits requires organizations to maintain thorough documentation of SOD policies, risk assessments, and audit findings. Compliance teams must work closely with IT and security departments to ensure that all necessary controls are in place and that audit reports are readily available for review.

Continuous improvement is essential for maintaining the effectiveness of SOD risk assessments and audits. Organizations must regularly update their SOD policies and access control frameworks to adapt to evolving security threats, business changes, and regulatory requirements. Periodic risk assessments should incorporate new access control technologies, automation capabilities, and threat intelligence to enhance SOD enforcement. Organizations should also provide ongoing training and awareness programs to educate employees on the importance of SOD compliance and how to recognize potential access conflicts. By fostering a culture of security awareness, organizations can ensure that SOD policies are consistently followed and that employees actively participate in maintaining compliance.

Remediation strategies are an integral part of SOD risk management, ensuring that identified conflicts are addressed in a timely manner. Organizations must establish clear procedures for resolving access conflicts, including role reassignments, access revocations, and policy adjustments. In some cases, compensating controls such as additional approvals, transaction monitoring, and periodic reviews may be implemented as temporary measures while permanent solutions are developed. Automated remediation workflows integrated with IAM solutions help organizations enforce corrective actions efficiently by automatically revoking conflicting access rights or escalating remediation tasks to the appropriate stakeholders.

Effective SOD risk assessments and audits provide organizations with the necessary visibility, control, and accountability to enforce access governance and prevent security incidents. By leveraging automation, analytics, and continuous monitoring, organizations can proactively identify and mitigate SOD violations, ensuring that access controls remain robust and aligned with business objectives. Conducting regular assessments and audits not only strengthens security but also supports regulatory compliance, reduces operational risks, and enhances overall trust in business processes.

Continuous Monitoring of SOD Policies

Continuous monitoring of Segregation of Duties (SOD) policies is essential for maintaining a strong security posture, preventing fraud, and ensuring regulatory compliance. While the initial implementation of SOD policies helps organizations establish necessary access controls, continuous monitoring ensures that these policies remain effective over time. Without ongoing oversight, access violations, policy misconfigurations, and security breaches can go undetected, leading to financial loss, compliance failures, and reputational damage. Continuous monitoring provides real-time visibility into user activities, access changes, and policy enforcement, enabling organizations to identify and remediate SOD violations before they escalate into serious risks.

Effective continuous monitoring begins with establishing real-time tracking of user access rights and role assignments. Identity and Access Management (IAM) solutions play a crucial role in automating the monitoring process by continuously evaluating user permissions against SOD policies. These solutions integrate with enterprise applications, cloud platforms, and privileged access management (PAM) systems to provide a centralized view of access control configurations. By automatically detecting conflicts in role assignments, IAM tools help security teams prevent unauthorized privilege escalations that could lead to policy violations. Organizations can configure real-time alerts to notify administrators when an employee is granted conflicting permissions or attempts to bypass approval workflows.

User activity monitoring is another critical component of continuous SOD enforcement. Organizations must track how employees interact with business applications, databases, and critical systems to ensure compliance with established access policies. Security Information and Event Management (SIEM) solutions enhance monitoring efforts by aggregating access logs from multiple sources and analyzing them for suspicious behavior. Machine learning and artificial intelligence-driven anomaly detection further strengthen monitoring capabilities by identifying deviations from normal access patterns. For example, if an employee suddenly gains access to financial approval functions outside of their normal role, an automated alert can be triggered for security review. By continuously monitoring user activities, organizations can detect unauthorized transactions, policy violations, and potential insider threats.

Privileged access monitoring is particularly important for enforcing SOD policies in IT environments. Administrative users and system operators have elevated privileges that could be misused to bypass security controls. PAM solutions help organizations enforce least privilege access by providing just-in-time (JIT) privilege escalation and session recording. Continuous monitoring of privileged access ensures that administrators do not perform unauthorized modifications, disable security controls, or create hidden backdoor accounts. By recording all privileged sessions and maintaining audit trails, organizations can verify that administrative activities align with SOD policies and compliance requirements.

Cloud environments present additional challenges in continuous SOD monitoring due to their dynamic and decentralized nature. As organizations adopt multi-cloud and hybrid cloud infrastructures, they must ensure that SOD policies are enforced consistently across all platforms. Cloud-native monitoring solutions, such as Cloud Security Posture Management (CSPM) and Cloud Access Security Brokers (CASB), provide visibility into cloud access permissions, user activities, and policy enforcement. These solutions continuously assess cloud configurations for SOD violations, detecting unauthorized privilege escalations or misconfigurations that could expose sensitive data. Automated remediation workflows help organizations quickly respond to SOD conflicts in cloud environments by revoking excessive privileges or enforcing access restrictions.

Third-party access monitoring is another crucial aspect of continuous SOD enforcement. Many organizations rely on external vendors, contractors, and business partners who require temporary access to corporate systems. Without proper monitoring, third-party users may retain access beyond their required period, increasing the risk of security breaches. Organizations must implement continuous monitoring of third-party access by enforcing time-limited permissions, requiring multi-factor authentication (MFA), and tracking vendor activities. Automated access reviews ensure that third-party accounts are promptly deactivated when no longer needed, reducing exposure to security risks associated with external access.

Organizations must also incorporate risk-based monitoring to prioritize SOD enforcement efforts. Not all access conflicts carry the same level of risk, so organizations should classify and prioritize monitoring activities based on potential impact. High-risk areas such as financial transactions, payroll processing, and regulatory reporting require stricter controls and more frequent monitoring. Automated risk assessment models can help organizations determine which SOD violations pose the greatest threats and require immediate remediation. By applying a risk-based approach, organizations can allocate monitoring resources more effectively and focus on the most critical areas of compliance and security.

Continuous auditing complements monitoring efforts by providing organizations with regular assessments of SOD policy effectiveness. Automated audit logs maintain a historical record of access changes, policy violations, and remediation actions, allowing compliance teams to review policy adherence over time. Scheduled access certification campaigns ensure that users do not accumulate conflicting privileges and that SOD controls remain aligned with business requirements. Security teams can conduct periodic forensic analysis of audit logs to identify long-term trends in policy violations and adjust monitoring strategies accordingly. Automated reporting tools generate compliance documentation that can be used for regulatory audits and internal security reviews.

Automated enforcement mechanisms play a vital role in continuous SOD monitoring by preventing unauthorized access modifications in real time. Organizations can implement policy-based access controls that automatically reject access requests that violate SOD policies. For example, if an employee requests access to a system that conflicts with their current role, the IAM system can deny the request without requiring manual intervention. Adaptive access control mechanisms further enhance security by dynamically adjusting permissions based on user behavior, risk levels, and contextual attributes. By leveraging automation, organizations can reduce reliance on manual reviews and strengthen the integrity of SOD enforcement.

Employee education and awareness programs should be integrated into continuous SOD monitoring efforts to ensure that users understand the importance of compliance. Security training sessions should educate employees on recognizing SOD violations, reporting suspicious activities, and following proper access request procedures. Self-service access request portals with built-in SOD validation help employees understand why certain access requests may be denied and how to escalate legitimate exceptions. A culture of accountability and security awareness ensures that employees actively participate in maintaining SOD compliance, reducing the likelihood of accidental policy violations.

Organizations must also ensure that continuous SOD monitoring remains adaptable to evolving security threats and business changes. As new applications, systems, and business processes are introduced, SOD policies must be regularly updated to reflect these changes. Continuous monitoring solutions should be configured to automatically detect new access risks as they emerge, allowing organizations to respond quickly to security challenges. Threat intelligence integration further enhances monitoring efforts by correlating SOD violations with external threat indicators, helping organizations identify potential cyberattacks or insider threats.

By implementing continuous monitoring of SOD policies, organizations can maintain stronger access controls, reduce the risk of fraud and compliance violations, and improve overall security posture. Automated tracking of user activities, real-time policy enforcement, privileged access monitoring, risk-based prioritization, and ongoing auditing create a proactive security framework that ensures SOD policies remain effective over time. As regulatory requirements evolve and security threats become more sophisticated, continuous monitoring provides organizations with the agility needed to enforce access governance and mitigate emerging risks effectively.

SOD Conflict Management Strategies

Segregation of Duties (SOD) is a critical security and compliance measure that prevents conflicts of interest, fraud, and unauthorized access within an organization. However, despite the implementation of SOD policies, conflicts can still arise due to business changes, evolving roles, or misconfigurations in access management. Organizations must have a structured approach to managing SOD conflicts to ensure that access risks are minimized while maintaining operational efficiency. Effective conflict management strategies involve identifying SOD violations, assessing risks, implementing compensating controls, automating conflict resolution, and continuously monitoring user access to prevent policy breaches.

The first step in managing SOD conflicts is to identify and analyze conflicting access rights across the organization. Organizations must conduct a thorough review of their business processes, access controls, and role assignments to detect users who may have excessive or conflicting privileges. Identity and Access Management (IAM) solutions provide automated tools for conflict detection by scanning user roles and permissions across enterprise systems. These solutions compare existing access configurations against predefined SOD policies to highlight potential conflicts. For example, an employee with both procurement approval and payment processing privileges in an Enterprise Resource Planning (ERP) system would be flagged as a high-risk SOD violation. Once conflicts are identified, organizations can take corrective actions to address them before they lead to security breaches or compliance failures.

Risk assessment plays a crucial role in determining the severity of SOD conflicts and prioritizing their resolution. Not all access conflicts pose the same level of risk, so organizations must evaluate the potential impact of each conflict based on factors such as financial exposure, data sensitivity, regulatory implications, and the likelihood of misuse. High-risk conflicts, such as those involving financial transactions or privileged IT access, require immediate remediation, while lower-risk conflicts may be addressed through periodic reviews or compensating controls. Risk-based conflict management ensures that resources are allocated efficiently, focusing on resolving the most critical SOD violations first.

Implementing compensating controls is a key strategy for managing SOD conflicts without disrupting business operations. In some cases, strict segregation may not be feasible due to operational constraints, such as limited personnel in smaller teams or urgent business needs requiring temporary access. Compensating controls serve as alternative security measures that mitigate the risks associated with SOD conflicts. These controls may include enhanced monitoring, dual approvals, transaction logging, automated alerts, or time-limited access permissions. For example, if an employee must temporarily assume conflicting roles, a compensating control such as requiring a secondary manager's approval for transactions can reduce the risk of fraud or unauthorized activity. By implementing compensating controls, organizations can maintain security and compliance while allowing necessary flexibility in business operations.

Automating SOD conflict resolution improves efficiency and accuracy in managing access risks. Manual conflict resolution processes can be time-consuming and prone to errors, making it difficult to enforce SOD policies consistently across an organization. Automated IAM solutions help organizations resolve conflicts by enforcing policy-based access controls, automatically revoking conflicting permissions, and generating alerts for security teams to review. Access request workflows integrated with IAM systems ensure that conflicting access requests are either blocked or escalated for approval before being granted. Automated conflict resolution reduces administrative workload, enhances compliance, and minimizes human error in managing SOD violations.

Privileged Access Management (PAM) is another critical component of SOD conflict management, particularly for IT administrators and high-risk users. Privileged accounts have elevated access rights that can override standard access controls, making them potential targets for insider threats and cyberattacks. Organizations must enforce strict policies around privileged access, ensuring that SOD conflicts are identified and mitigated. PAM solutions help manage privileged users by enforcing just-in-time (JIT) access, requiring approvals before elevated permissions are granted, and monitoring all privileged activities through session recording. By integrating PAM with SOD conflict management strategies, organizations can ensure that administrative privileges are controlled and audited effectively.

Regular access reviews and certification campaigns are essential for maintaining SOD compliance and identifying new conflicts. Organizations must conduct periodic access audits to verify that users do not accumulate conflicting privileges over time. Access reviews involve analyzing current role assignments, validating permissions against SOD policies, and revoking unnecessary or excessive access rights. IAM tools automate access reviews by generating reports that highlight SOD violations and providing workflows for managers to approve or remove conflicting access. By continuously reviewing user access, organizations can prevent privilege creep and maintain compliance with regulatory requirements.

Exception handling is an important aspect of SOD conflict management, allowing organizations to address temporary access conflicts while maintaining security oversight. There may be scenarios where employees require exceptions to SOD policies due to business requirements, role transitions, or emergency situations. Organizations must establish clear exception management processes that define when and how temporary SOD conflicts can be granted. Exception approvals should involve multiple stakeholders, such as security teams, compliance officers, and department heads, to ensure that risks are properly evaluated. All exceptions should be time-bound, closely monitored, and documented to ensure that temporary access does not become permanent.

Continuous monitoring of SOD policies helps organizations detect and prevent conflicts before they escalate into security incidents. Real-time monitoring solutions track user activities, access changes, and policy violations across enterprise systems. SIEM (Security Information and Event Management) platforms analyze log data to identify suspicious behavior, such as unauthorized privilege escalation or repeated access attempts to restricted functions. AI-driven anomaly detection further enhances continuous monitoring by identifying deviations from normal access patterns. Automated alerts and remediation actions ensure that security teams can respond promptly to SOD violations, minimizing the risk of financial loss or data breaches.

Integrating SOD conflict management with compliance frameworks ensures that organizations meet regulatory requirements and industry standards. Many regulations, such as the Sarbanes-Oxley Act (SOX), the General Data Protection Regulation (GDPR), and the Payment Card Industry Data Security Standard (PCI DSS), mandate strict access controls to prevent fraud and unauthorized activities. Organizations must document their SOD conflict management processes, maintain audit logs of policy enforcement, and provide evidence of compliance during regulatory audits. Automated compliance reporting tools generate detailed reports on SOD violations, access changes, and remediation actions, helping organizations demonstrate adherence to security policies.

Training and awareness programs support effective SOD conflict management by ensuring that employees understand access control policies and their role in maintaining compliance. Organizations should provide regular training sessions on SOD principles, access request procedures, and the importance of preventing conflicts of interest. Security awareness programs help employees recognize and report potential access conflicts, reducing the likelihood of accidental policy violations. By fostering a culture of compliance, organizations can strengthen their overall security posture and ensure that employees actively participate in maintaining SOD enforcement.

As business environments evolve, organizations must continuously refine their SOD conflict management strategies to address emerging security threats and access risks. By implementing automated conflict detection, risk-based prioritization, compensating controls, privileged access restrictions, continuous monitoring, and compliance alignment, organizations can effectively manage SOD conflicts while maintaining operational efficiency. A proactive approach to SOD conflict management ensures that access controls remain strong, policy violations are promptly addressed, and organizations stay compliant with industry regulations and security best practices.

SOD in Cloud-Based IAM Solutions

As organizations continue to migrate to cloud environments, enforcing Segregation of Duties (SOD) within cloud-based Identity and Access Management (IAM) solutions has become increasingly complex. Traditional SOD enforcement strategies, which were originally designed for on-premises infrastructures, often do not translate directly to the dynamic and distributed nature of cloud platforms. Cloud-based IAM introduces new challenges such as decentralized access control, rapid privilege escalations, and increased reliance on third-party integrations. Organizations must adapt their SOD frameworks to accommodate the flexibility and scalability of cloud environments while ensuring that security, compliance, and operational integrity remain intact.

One of the fundamental aspects of implementing SOD in cloud-based IAM solutions is defining clear role-based access control (RBAC) structures that align with business requirements and security policies. Cloud platforms such as Amazon Web Services (AWS), Microsoft Azure, and Google Cloud Platform (GCP) provide IAM capabilities that allow organizations to define user roles and assign permissions. However, without proper governance, users may accumulate excessive privileges over time, leading to conflicts of interest and SOD violations. Organizations must establish and enforce policies that prevent users from having access to conflicting functions, such as managing both identity provisioning and access approval within the same cloud environment. By carefully mapping cloud-specific roles and ensuring that high-risk permissions are segregated, organizations can reduce the likelihood of privilege abuse.

Attribute-Based Access Control (ABAC) plays a crucial role in enhancing SOD enforcement within cloud-based IAM solutions. Unlike RBAC, which relies on static role assignments, ABAC uses contextual attributes such as user location, department, job title, and time of access to make real-time access control decisions. This dynamic approach is particularly beneficial in cloud environments where user access needs frequently change. For example, an organization can configure an ABAC policy to prevent a user from initiating financial transactions and approving them within the same system, even if they have different roles assigned across multiple cloud applications. By leveraging ABAC, organizations can enforce SOD policies in a more granular and adaptable manner across cloud platforms.

Cloud-based IAM solutions also introduce the challenge of managing cross-cloud access, where users require permissions across multiple cloud providers and Software-as-a-Service (SaaS) applications. Organizations using multi-cloud environments must ensure that SOD policies are consistently enforced across all platforms. Without centralized governance, users may unintentionally gain conflicting privileges in different cloud systems, increasing security risks. Identity federation and single sign-on (SSO) solutions help mitigate this issue by providing a unified identity management framework that enforces consistent access policies across various cloud environments. By integrating SSO with cloud IAM platforms, organizations can apply SOD rules across multiple domains, preventing unauthorized privilege escalations.

Privileged Access Management (PAM) is essential for SOD enforcement in cloud-based IAM solutions, as privileged users often have broad access to cloud resources. Cloud environments typically rely on automation tools, such as Infrastructure-as-Code (IaC) scripts, to manage provisioning and configuration. If privileged accounts are not properly controlled, they can lead to unauthorized changes, data breaches, or compliance violations. Cloud-based PAM solutions provide just-in-time (JIT) privileged access, ensuring that administrative privileges are granted only for a limited time and only when necessary. Additionally, session recording and audit logging ensure that all privileged actions are tracked, helping organizations detect and remediate potential SOD violations.

Automated SOD conflict detection is a key feature of modern cloud IAM solutions, enabling organizations to continuously analyze user permissions and detect policy violations. Cloud-native security tools use artificial intelligence (AI) and machine learning (ML) to identify patterns of privilege accumulation, role conflicts, and unauthorized access attempts. For example, if a cloud user gains access to both billing approval and invoice processing functions, an AI-driven IAM system can automatically flag the conflict and initiate a remediation workflow. By integrating automated conflict detection into cloud IAM solutions, organizations can proactively prevent SOD violations before they lead to security incidents.

Continuous monitoring of SOD policies is critical in cloud-based IAM environments, where user access changes frequently and new permissions are granted dynamically. Cloud security posture management (CSPM) solutions provide real-time monitoring of access controls, helping organizations enforce SOD policies across cloud platforms. These solutions analyze cloud configurations, detect policy deviations, and provide remediation recommendations to ensure that users do not accumulate conflicting privileges over time. Additionally, Security Information and Event Management (SIEM) systems can integrate with cloud IAM tools to provide centralized logging, alerting, and forensic analysis of SOD violations. By continuously monitoring user access and privilege changes, organizations can maintain strict enforcement of SOD policies in the cloud.

Regulatory compliance is another major factor driving the need for robust SOD enforcement in cloud-based IAM solutions. Many industry regulations, including the General Data Protection Regulation (GDPR), the Sarbanes-Oxley Act (SOX), and the Payment Card Industry Data Security Standard (PCI DSS), require organizations to implement access controls that prevent unauthorized transactions and data exposure. Cloud-based IAM solutions must include automated reporting and audit capabilities to demonstrate compliance with these regulatory requirements. Organizations must ensure that SOD policies align with legal mandates and that access control logs are readily available for external audits. Compliance automation tools help organizations generate audit-ready reports, reducing the burden of manual compliance tracking.

Organizations must also implement third-party access controls to prevent SOD violations resulting from external vendors, contractors, and business partners who require cloud access. Without proper oversight, third-party users may be granted excessive privileges that allow them to bypass SOD policies. Cloud-based IAM solutions should enforce strict access governance for third parties by implementing zero-trust principles, time-restricted access, and multi-factor authentication (MFA). Additionally, organizations should regularly review third-party access permissions and revoke unnecessary privileges to minimize security risks. By applying rigorous controls to external users, organizations can reduce the likelihood of SOD violations caused by third-party access.

Training and awareness programs are essential for ensuring that employees understand the importance of SOD enforcement in cloud-based IAM solutions. Organizations must educate IT administrators, security teams, and business users on cloud-specific access risks, policy enforcement strategies, and compliance requirements. Training programs should cover best practices for requesting access, managing privileged accounts, and recognizing potential SOD violations. Security awareness initiatives help build a culture of compliance, ensuring that employees adhere to SOD policies and report suspicious activities related to cloud access.

As organizations continue to expand their cloud adoption, SOD enforcement in cloud-based IAM solutions must evolve to address new security challenges. By implementing role-based and attribute-based access controls, integrating PAM and AI-driven conflict detection, continuously monitoring access changes, ensuring regulatory compliance, managing third-party risks, and educating employees on security best practices, organizations can strengthen their SOD frameworks in cloud environments. A proactive and automated approach to SOD enforcement ensures that organizations maintain security, prevent fraud, and comply with regulatory requirements while leveraging the benefits of cloud computing.

SOD in Hybrid and Multi-Cloud Environments

As organizations increasingly adopt hybrid and multi-cloud environments to enhance scalability, flexibility, and operational efficiency, enforcing Segregation of Duties (SOD) in these complex infrastructures presents significant challenges. Hybrid environments combine on-premises systems with cloud services, while multi-cloud environments distribute workloads across multiple cloud providers such as Amazon Web Services (AWS), Microsoft Azure, and Google Cloud Platform (GCP). In these decentralized ecosystems, ensuring that users do not accumulate conflicting privileges across various platforms becomes a critical security concern. Organizations must develop a comprehensive strategy to enforce SOD consistently, prevent unauthorized access, and mitigate the risks of privilege escalation across hybrid and multi-cloud environments.

One of the biggest challenges in enforcing SOD across hybrid and multi-cloud environments is the lack of centralized identity and access management. In traditional on-premises IT environments, access controls are managed through a single directory service, such as Active Directory (AD) or LDAP. However, in cloud and hybrid setups, users often have accounts across multiple identity providers, SaaS applications, and cloud platforms, leading to fragmented access control. Without a unified IAM strategy, users may inadvertently accumulate conflicting permissions across different systems, violating SOD policies. Organizations must implement federated identity management solutions and single sign-on (SSO) to centralize authentication and enforce consistent SOD policies across all platforms.

Role-Based Access Control (RBAC) is a fundamental approach to enforcing SOD in hybrid and multi-cloud environments, but it requires careful alignment across different platforms. Each cloud provider has its own IAM framework with unique role structures and permission models. AWS IAM, Azure RBAC, and Google Cloud IAM operate differently, making it challenging to maintain uniform SOD policies. Organizations must map roles consistently across all platforms to ensure that users do not inadvertently gain excessive privileges. For example, an administrator with financial approval rights in an on-premises ERP system should not have payment processing privileges in a cloud-based finance application. Aligning RBAC policies across hybrid environments helps prevent such conflicts and enforces SOD effectively.

Attribute-Based Access Control (ABAC) provides a more dynamic and adaptable approach to SOD enforcement in hybrid and multi-cloud environments. Unlike RBAC, which assigns static roles, ABAC evaluates real-time attributes such as job function, department, location, and device security posture to determine access permissions. This flexibility is particularly useful in hybrid environments where users require temporary access to cloud resources while maintaining on-premises responsibilities. By implementing ABAC, organizations can enforce context-aware SOD policies, ensuring that users cannot perform conflicting duties based on their contextual attributes. For example, a cloud engineer working from an unmanaged device may be restricted from modifying security configurations even if they hold an administrative role.

Privileged Access Management (PAM) is essential for SOD enforcement in hybrid and multi-cloud environments, where privileged users often have broad access across multiple platforms. Cloud administrators, DevOps engineers, and IT security personnel frequently require elevated permissions to manage cloud workloads, configure infrastructure, and deploy applications. Without proper governance, these privileged users may bypass SOD policies, leading to security risks. PAM solutions enforce just-in-time (JIT) privileged access, requiring approvals before granting elevated permissions. Additionally, PAM tools provide session recording, audit logging, and real-time monitoring to ensure that privileged activities comply with SOD policies. By integrating PAM across hybrid and multi-cloud environments, organizations can mitigate the risks associated with privileged access while enforcing SOD controls.

Automating SOD conflict detection is crucial in hybrid and multi-cloud environments due to the dynamic nature of access provisioning. Traditional manual reviews of access rights are insufficient in cloud environments, where permissions can be modified rapidly. Organizations should implement AI-driven IAM solutions that continuously analyze access privileges across different platforms and detect SOD violations in real time. These solutions use machine learning to identify role conflicts, privilege escalations, and unauthorized access attempts. If an employee gains conflicting permissions across multiple cloud environments, automated remediation workflows can revoke access or require additional approvals. AI-driven conflict detection reduces human error and strengthens SOD enforcement in complex IT ecosystems.

Continuous monitoring and logging are vital for maintaining SOD compliance in hybrid and multi-cloud environments. Security teams must track user activity across all cloud platforms, logging every access request, privilege escalation, and transaction approval. SIEM (Security Information and Event Management) solutions integrate with IAM systems to aggregate log data and provide real-time threat detection. By correlating access events across on-premises and cloud environments, SIEM tools help identify suspicious behavior that may indicate SOD violations. For example, if an employee attempts to override approval workflows in multiple systems, security teams can receive alerts and take immediate action. Automated alerting and forensic analysis ensure that organizations maintain visibility into SOD enforcement and respond to potential risks proactively.

Cloud security posture management (CSPM) solutions provide an additional layer of protection by continuously assessing cloud configurations for compliance with SOD policies. These tools identify misconfigurations, excessive permissions, and access anomalies that could lead to SOD violations. For example, a CSPM solution may detect that a database administrator has unauthorized access to encryption keys, which could allow them to bypass data security controls. By integrating CSPM with IAM solutions, organizations can enforce SOD policies dynamically, ensuring that cloud configurations adhere to security best practices.

Regulatory compliance requirements further drive the need for strict SOD enforcement in hybrid and multi-cloud environments. Organizations operating under frameworks such as the General Data Protection Regulation (GDPR), the Sarbanes-Oxley Act (SOX), and the Payment Card Industry Data Security Standard (PCI DSS) must ensure that access controls prevent unauthorized transactions and data exposure. Cloud-based IAM solutions must support compliance automation by generating audit reports, tracking policy violations, and providing real-time compliance dashboards. Organizations should establish standardized audit procedures to ensure that SOD policies are enforced consistently across all cloud providers and on-premises systems.

Third-party access management presents another challenge for SOD enforcement in hybrid and multi-cloud environments. Many organizations rely on external vendors, contractors, and service providers who require temporary access to cloud platforms and enterprise applications. Without proper governance, third-party users may receive excessive privileges that violate SOD policies. Organizations must implement zero-trust principles, time-limited access controls, and continuous monitoring for third-party users. Automated access reviews ensure that third-party accounts are deactivated when no longer needed, reducing the risk of unauthorized access. By applying strict third-party access governance, organizations can prevent SOD violations while maintaining security and compliance.

Security awareness and training programs are essential for ensuring that employees understand the importance of SOD enforcement in hybrid and multi-cloud environments. Organizations must educate IT administrators, cloud security teams, and business users on best practices for managing cloud access, recognizing privilege escalation risks, and adhering to compliance requirements. Employees should be trained on how to request access properly, follow approval workflows, and report suspicious activities. A strong culture of security awareness ensures that users actively participate in maintaining SOD compliance.

As organizations expand their hybrid and multi-cloud strategies, they must adopt a proactive approach to SOD enforcement. By implementing federated identity management, leveraging ABAC for dynamic access control, integrating PAM for privileged user governance, automating SOD conflict detection, and continuously monitoring cloud access, organizations can strengthen their SOD frameworks. Aligning IAM strategies with regulatory compliance requirements and applying strict third-party access controls further enhances security. A well-defined SOD enforcement strategy in hybrid and multi-cloud environments ensures that organizations maintain operational integrity, prevent unauthorized access, and mitigate security risks in an increasingly complex digital landscape.

Leveraging AI and Machine Learning for SOD Controls

The adoption of artificial intelligence (AI) and machine learning (ML) in Identity and Access Management (IAM) is transforming the enforcement of Segregation of Duties (SOD) policies. Traditional SOD controls rely on static rule-based mechanisms that require manual oversight, making them inefficient, error-prone, and difficult to scale in complex IT environments. AI and ML introduce automation, intelligence, and adaptability to SOD enforcement, enabling organizations to detect violations in real-time, predict potential access risks, and strengthen compliance with regulatory frameworks. By leveraging AI and ML for SOD controls, organizations can improve access governance, reduce fraud, and enhance operational security across cloud, hybrid, and on-premises environments.

One of the most significant benefits of AI-driven SOD enforcement is the ability to automate conflict detection across large-scale enterprise environments. Traditional SOD audits involve manually reviewing access privileges, role assignments, and approval workflows to identify policy violations. This approach is labor-intensive and fails to keep up with the rapid pace of access changes in dynamic IT ecosystems. AI-driven IAM solutions analyze access patterns in real-time, continuously scanning for conflicts that could lead to unauthorized transactions or privilege escalations. Machine learning models detect access anomalies by identifying users who have gained conflicting permissions across multiple systems, flagging these issues for immediate remediation.

AI and ML enhance role mining and optimization, a critical component of SOD policy enforcement. Organizations often struggle with excessive role accumulation and privilege creep, where employees retain access to systems they no longer need. This leads to unintended

SOD violations as users accumulate permissions that create conflicts. AI-driven role mining tools analyze historical access data, user behavior, and transaction patterns to identify optimal role structures. Machine learning algorithms classify users based on their actual access needs, recommending streamlined roles that eliminate excessive privileges while maintaining operational efficiency. By continuously refining role assignments, organizations can enforce SOD policies more effectively and prevent role-based access conflicts.

Predictive risk assessment is another key advantage of leveraging AI and ML for SOD controls. Traditional access control mechanisms operate reactively, detecting policy violations only after they occur. AI-powered risk models take a proactive approach by assessing the likelihood of an SOD violation before it happens. Machine learning algorithms evaluate contextual factors such as login behavior, access frequency, transaction history, and device security posture to calculate risk scores for each user. If a user exhibits high-risk behavior, such as attempting to gain conflicting privileges or accessing unauthorized systems, AI-driven IAM solutions can trigger automated preventive actions such as requiring additional approvals, enforcing multi-factor authentication (MFA), or temporarily restricting access.

AI-driven anomaly detection improves SOD monitoring by identifying suspicious access behavior that deviates from normal patterns. Machine learning models continuously learn from user activities, recognizing expected workflows and flagging deviations that may indicate unauthorized actions. For example, if an employee in the finance department typically processes purchase orders but suddenly attempts to modify financial records, the system detects this as an anomaly and generates an alert. Unlike static rule-based monitoring, AI-powered detection adapts to evolving threats, allowing organizations to identify insider threats, credential abuse, and fraud attempts in real-time. Automated alerts enable security teams to investigate and respond to potential SOD violations before they lead to data breaches or financial loss.

Privileged access management (PAM) is a critical area where AI and ML significantly enhance SOD enforcement. Privileged users, such as system administrators and security engineers, have elevated permissions that can bypass traditional access controls. AI-driven PAM solutions analyze privileged user behavior to detect unusual activities, such as unauthorized privilege escalations or excessive access requests. Machine learning models establish baseline behavior profiles for privileged users, identifying deviations that could indicate compromised credentials or insider threats. By integrating AI with PAM, organizations can implement adaptive access controls that dynamically adjust privileged access permissions based on real-time risk assessments, ensuring compliance with SOD policies.

Automating access certification and recertification processes using AI reduces the administrative burden of periodic reviews while strengthening SOD enforcement. Traditional access reviews involve managers manually verifying user permissions, often leading to oversight due to the complexity of evaluating access across multiple applications. AI-powered access governance platforms automate this process by analyzing user access data, highlighting high-risk role conflicts, and recommending corrective actions. Machine learning models prioritize access reviews based on risk levels, ensuring that security teams focus on the most critical SOD violations first. Automated workflows streamline access certifications, reducing human error and improving compliance with regulatory standards.

AI-driven IAM solutions enhance compliance auditing by providing automated reporting and real-time insights into SOD enforcement. Regulations such as the Sarbanes-Oxley Act (SOX), the General Data Protection Regulation (GDPR), and the Payment Card Industry Data Security Standard (PCI DSS) require strict access controls and periodic audits to prevent fraud and unauthorized transactions. AI-powered compliance dashboards provide security teams with visibility into access control violations, remediation actions, and policy adherence across the organization. Natural language processing (NLP) capabilities allow auditors to generate detailed reports and query access logs using conversational AI, simplifying compliance assessments. By automating compliance tracking, organizations reduce audit preparation time and minimize the risk of regulatory penalties.

AI and ML also improve the handling of exception requests in SOD enforcement. Employees occasionally require temporary access to conflicting roles due to project-based tasks, emergencies, or role transitions. Traditional SOD enforcement mechanisms often rely on rigid access control policies that either block access entirely or require lengthy approval processes. AI-driven exception management systems evaluate the risk of temporary access requests based on contextual attributes and behavioral analysis. If a user requests conflicting access for a valid reason, the system can enforce compensating controls such as additional approvals, increased transaction monitoring, or session recording. This approach ensures that business needs are met while maintaining SOD compliance and reducing security risks.

Continuous learning and adaptation are fundamental to AI-driven SOD controls, allowing organizations to evolve their access control policies based on emerging threats and user behavior. Machine learning models continuously refine their understanding of access risks by analyzing real-world security incidents, identifying new patterns of privilege abuse, and recommending updates to SOD policies. AI-driven threat intelligence platforms integrate with IAM solutions to correlate access control violations with external cyber threats, providing organizations with proactive defense mechanisms against evolving attack vectors. By leveraging continuous learning, organizations can enhance the accuracy and effectiveness of SOD enforcement over time.

As enterprises continue to expand their digital transformation efforts, AI and ML will play an increasingly vital role in strengthening SOD controls across cloud, hybrid, and on-premises environments. By automating conflict detection, optimizing role management, enabling predictive risk assessments, enhancing privileged access monitoring, streamlining compliance auditing, and improving exception handling, AI-driven IAM solutions provide organizations with the intelligence and automation needed to enforce SOD policies more effectively. The integration of AI-powered analytics and machine learning-driven security measures ensures that organizations can proactively detect, prevent, and remediate SOD violations, ultimately reducing fraud, enhancing compliance, and maintaining a robust security posture.

Role Mining and Role Engineering for SOD Compliance

Role mining and role engineering are fundamental processes in establishing and maintaining Segregation of Duties (SOD) compliance within an organization's Identity and Access Management (IAM) framework. As enterprises expand, employees, contractors, and third-party users require access to multiple systems and applications, leading to a complex web of access permissions. Without structured role management, organizations face challenges such as excessive privilege accumulation, access conflicts, and unauthorized actions that violate SOD policies. Role mining and role engineering provide a systematic approach to defining, analyzing, and optimizing role-based access control (RBAC) models, ensuring that users receive only the necessary permissions while preventing conflicts of interest.

Role mining is the process of analyzing existing user access patterns to identify optimal role structures. This involves evaluating user permissions, access history, and application usage to detect commonalities and redundancies in access assignments. Organizations often accumulate access inconsistencies over time due to manual provisioning, role creep, and lack of periodic access reviews. Role mining helps uncover these inefficiencies and provides data-driven insights into how roles should be structured to align with business needs and security requirements. By leveraging automated tools, organizations can extract role patterns from historical data, detect unnecessary privileges, and create streamlined roles that enforce SOD compliance.

Role engineering is the process of designing, defining, and implementing role-based access control models based on business functions and security policies. Unlike role mining, which focuses on analyzing existing access assignments, role engineering takes a proactive approach by structuring roles according to business requirements and compliance regulations. Organizations must carefully define job functions, responsibilities, and access privileges to ensure that users do not have conflicting permissions. A well-structured role engineering framework establishes role hierarchies, enforces least privilege access, and prevents users from accumulating excessive permissions over time. By implementing role engineering best practices, organizations can maintain control over access management and ensure that SOD policies are enforced consistently.

One of the key challenges in role mining and role engineering for SOD compliance is identifying and mitigating role conflicts. Organizations must analyze role assignments to determine whether any users have conflicting duties that could lead to policy violations. For example, in financial systems, a user with access to both accounts payable and accounts receivable functions creates a risk of fraudulent transactions. Similarly, in IT security, an administrator who manages system configurations and audits security logs could potentially manipulate access records to conceal unauthorized changes. Role mining tools help detect these conflicts, allowing organizations to restructure roles and apply compensating controls to maintain compliance.

Automating role mining processes improves efficiency and accuracy in SOD enforcement. Traditional role analysis relies on manual reviews of access control lists, making it difficult to identify hidden role conflicts and privilege overlaps. AI-driven role mining solutions analyze large datasets, identify access patterns, and generate role recommendations based on real usage data. These solutions use machine learning algorithms to cluster users with similar access needs, eliminating unnecessary role assignments and reducing the risk of privilege escalation. By automating role mining, organizations can simplify role management, improve access control transparency, and ensure that SOD policies are enforced without human bias or oversight errors.

Role engineering also involves defining role hierarchies and inheritance structures to streamline access management. Organizations must establish parent-child relationships between roles to ensure that access control policies remain scalable and manageable. For example, a senior finance manager role may inherit access privileges from lower-level financial roles while still being subject to SOD restrictions. By structuring roles hierarchically, organizations can prevent excessive privilege accumulation while maintaining operational efficiency. Role-based inheritance models help organizations enforce SOD policies dynamically, ensuring that role assignments remain consistent across different business units and departments.

Role certification and periodic reviews play a crucial role in maintaining SOD compliance after role mining and engineering efforts have been completed. Organizations must continuously validate that role assignments align with business needs and security policies. IAM solutions provide automated role certification workflows that allow managers and compliance officers to review user access and verify that no unauthorized privileges have been granted. If an SOD conflict is detected during a role review, corrective actions such as access revocation, role modification, or compensating controls must be implemented to mitigate risk. Regular role certification helps organizations prevent access drift, where users retain outdated or unnecessary privileges due to role changes, job transfers, or department restructuring.

Integration with Attribute-Based Access Control (ABAC) enhances role engineering efforts by allowing organizations to apply dynamic access policies based on contextual attributes. Unlike RBAC, which assigns static roles, ABAC evaluates attributes such as job function, location, device security posture, and risk score before granting access. This flexibility is particularly useful for enforcing SOD policies in cloud environments, where access requirements frequently change. For example, an ABAC policy could prevent a user from accessing both procurement approvals and payment processing functions within the same session, even if they hold different roles in separate applications. By combining role engineering with ABAC, organizations can enforce SOD dynamically while maintaining operational agility.

Privileged Access Management (PAM) must also be considered in role engineering for SOD compliance. High-level administrative roles often have elevated privileges that could allow users to bypass SOD controls. Organizations must define separate privileged roles with limited access scopes, ensuring that administrators cannot perform conflicting tasks without oversight. PAM solutions enforce just-in-time (JIT) privileged access, requiring approvals before elevated permissions are granted. By incorporating PAM into role engineering strategies, organizations can enforce SOD principles while reducing the risks associated with privileged user access.

Cloud adoption and hybrid IT environments introduce additional challenges in role mining and role engineering for SOD compliance. Organizations must ensure that role structures are consistently enforced across on-premises applications, cloud platforms, and SaaS solutions. Cloud IAM tools provide centralized visibility into user roles, allowing organizations to map role assignments across different environments. Automated role synchronization ensures that users do not accumulate conflicting privileges in multiple cloud systems. By aligning cloud and on-premises role management strategies, organizations can enforce SOD policies consistently, regardless of where users access enterprise resources.

Training and awareness programs are essential for ensuring that employees and administrators understand the importance of SOD compliance in role management. Organizations must educate users on access control best practices, the risks of privilege accumulation, and the role review process. Security awareness training helps employees recognize potential role conflicts and understand how role mining and engineering contribute to overall security and compliance efforts. By fostering a culture of security, organizations can ensure that SOD policies are actively supported and upheld across all departments.

Role mining and role engineering provide a structured approach to enforcing SOD policies, improving access control efficiency, and reducing security risks. By leveraging automated tools, implementing hierarchical role structures, integrating ABAC and PAM, and conducting regular role certifications, organizations can maintain compliance with regulatory requirements while optimizing access governance. As enterprise environments continue to evolve, role management strategies must be continuously refined to address emerging access risks, ensuring that SOD controls remain effective in preventing unauthorized transactions and privilege abuse.

Handling Exceptions in SOD Policies

Segregation of Duties (SOD) policies are designed to ensure that no single individual has unchecked control over critical business functions. By separating key responsibilities among multiple individuals, organizations can prevent fraud, unauthorized transactions, and conflicts of interest. However, real-world business operations are often complex, requiring flexibility in access control mechanisms. There are situations where strict SOD enforcement may not be practical, and temporary or permanent exceptions to policies become necessary. Handling exceptions in SOD policies requires a structured approach to minimize risks while ensuring that necessary business functions continue without disruption. Organizations must implement well-defined processes for evaluating, approving, monitoring, and revoking SOD exceptions to maintain compliance and security.

One of the most common reasons for granting SOD exceptions is operational necessity. In smaller teams or specialized roles, employees may be required to perform multiple functions due to limited personnel. For example, in a startup or a small finance department, it may not be feasible to strictly separate financial transaction approvals from transaction processing. Similarly, in IT administration, an engineer responsible for maintaining a database may also need emergency access to logs for troubleshooting. These exceptions must be documented and reviewed carefully to ensure that they do not create unacceptable security risks.

Emergency situations also necessitate SOD exceptions, especially in IT and security operations. During system outages, cyber incidents, or urgent financial transactions, employees may need temporary elevated privileges to perform critical tasks. If strict SOD enforcement prevents rapid response, the organization could suffer operational downtime, financial penalties, or security breaches. To mitigate risks, emergency access should be time-restricted, closely monitored, and subject to retrospective review. Privileged Access Management (PAM) solutions provide just-in-time (JIT) privileged access, ensuring that emergency access is granted only when absolutely necessary and revoked once the crisis is resolved.

Another common scenario requiring SOD exceptions involves temporary staffing changes. Employees on leave, contractors, or interim managers may need access to multiple business functions to ensure continuity of operations. Without proper exception handling, granting these users excessive privileges can lead to SOD violations and security risks. Organizations must implement temporary access approval processes that include multi-level reviews and compensating controls. Access should be granted only for the minimum duration required, and all exceptions should be tracked in an audit log to ensure accountability.

Managing SOD exceptions requires a formalized approval workflow to prevent unauthorized privilege escalations. Exception requests should be documented and reviewed by multiple stakeholders, including security teams, compliance officers, and business managers. Organizations must define clear criteria for approving exceptions, such as the specific business justification, the duration of the exception, and any compensating controls that will be applied. Automated IAM workflows help streamline exception approvals, ensuring that requests are systematically evaluated based on predefined policies.

Compensating controls are critical in mitigating risks associated with SOD exceptions. When a user is granted conflicting privileges, additional security measures must be implemented to reduce the risk of unauthorized activities. Common compensating controls include requiring dual approvals for high-risk transactions, increasing logging and monitoring of user activities, and enforcing multi-factor authentication (MFA) for sensitive operations. For example, if an employee is granted temporary access to both procurement and payment processing systems, all transactions they initiate could require independent review by a senior manager. By implementing these controls, organizations can allow necessary exceptions while maintaining oversight and reducing security exposure.

Continuous monitoring of SOD exceptions is essential to prevent abuse and ensure compliance. Organizations must track all approved exceptions in an audit log, regularly reviewing whether they are still required. Security teams should monitor user activities for anomalies, such as excessive transactions, unusual login patterns, or repeated exception requests from the same users. SIEM (Security Information and Event Management) solutions integrate with IAM systems to detect suspicious behavior and trigger alerts when exceptions are misused. Machine learning-driven analytics can further enhance monitoring by identifying patterns that suggest fraudulent activities or policy violations.

Periodic access reviews are necessary to validate whether SOD exceptions should remain in place or be revoked. Organizations must establish review cycles, such as monthly or quarterly assessments, to evaluate all approved exceptions. Business managers and security teams should collaborate to determine if the original business justification for an exception is still valid. If an exception is no longer needed, access should be promptly revoked. IAM solutions provide automated access review tools that generate reports on active exceptions, highlighting those that require immediate attention. By conducting regular reviews, organizations can prevent temporary exceptions from becoming permanent security risks.

Regulatory compliance plays a significant role in how organizations handle SOD exceptions. Many industry regulations, including the Sarbanes-Oxley Act (SOX), the General Data Protection Regulation (GDPR), and the Payment Card Industry Data Security Standard (PCI DSS), mandate strict access controls to prevent fraud and unauthorized transactions. Auditors often scrutinize SOD policies, looking for unapproved privilege escalations or excessive exceptions that undermine security controls. Organizations must ensure that all SOD exceptions are well-documented, properly approved, and subject to continuous monitoring. Automated compliance reporting tools help organizations demonstrate that exceptions are managed responsibly and in alignment with regulatory requirements.

Training and awareness programs are crucial in ensuring that employees understand the importance of SOD policies and the proper procedures for requesting exceptions. Many SOD violations occur due to a lack of awareness rather than malicious intent. Employees must be educated on access control best practices, the risks of privilege accumulation, and the steps required to obtain temporary access approvals. Security teams should conduct regular training sessions to reinforce the importance of SOD compliance and encourage employees to report potential policy violations. A strong security culture helps prevent unnecessary exceptions and ensures that users follow proper access request protocols.

Technology solutions play a vital role in streamlining SOD exception handling. IAM platforms with built-in policy enforcement mechanisms can automatically detect access conflicts and prevent unauthorized privilege escalations. PAM solutions provide controlled, time-limited privileged access that minimizes security risks. AI-driven analytics enhance exception management by identifying high-risk users and predicting potential fraud attempts. By leveraging automation and intelligence, organizations can reduce administrative overhead while maintaining strict control over SOD exceptions.

Organizations must continuously refine their SOD exception handling processes to adapt to evolving business needs and security threats. By implementing structured approval workflows, enforcing compensating controls, conducting continuous monitoring, and aligning with compliance requirements, organizations can effectively manage exceptions without compromising security. A well-defined exception management strategy ensures that SOD policies remain enforceable while allowing necessary flexibility for business operations.

SOD in DevOps and Agile Environments

Segregation of Duties (SOD) is a foundational security principle that prevents conflicts of interest, unauthorized access, and fraud by ensuring that critical tasks are distributed among multiple individuals. While SOD has traditionally been enforced in structured IT and business environments, its application in DevOps and Agile environments presents unique challenges. DevOps emphasizes speed, collaboration, automation, and continuous integration and deployment, while Agile development promotes flexibility and rapid iteration. These methodologies often blur the lines between development, testing, deployment, and operational responsibilities, potentially leading to violations of traditional SOD principles. Organizations must adapt their SOD enforcement strategies to accommodate the fast-paced and decentralized nature of DevOps and Agile workflows while maintaining security and compliance.

One of the primary challenges of implementing SOD in DevOps is the consolidation of responsibilities within small, cross-functional teams. In traditional IT environments, developers write code, testers validate it, and operations teams deploy and maintain it. However, in DevOps, a single engineer may be responsible for writing code, testing it, deploying it, and managing infrastructure through Infrastructure-as-Code (IaC) tools. This level of role consolidation increases the risk of unauthorized changes, undetected vulnerabilities, and compliance failures. To mitigate these risks, organizations must define role-based access controls (RBAC) that ensure no single individual has unrestricted control over the entire software development lifecycle.

Automated pipelines in DevOps environments introduce another complexity in SOD enforcement. Continuous Integration and Continuous Deployment (CI/CD) pipelines automate the process of building, testing, and deploying applications, reducing human intervention but also introducing security risks. If these pipelines are not properly governed, a developer with excessive privileges could bypass security controls, inject malicious code, or deploy unauthorized changes directly into production. Organizations must implement SOD controls within CI/CD pipelines by requiring peer code reviews, automated security scans, and approval workflows before deployment. Role segregation should be enforced at every stage of the pipeline to ensure that different individuals or automated processes are responsible for coding, testing, approving, and deploying software.

Privileged access management (PAM) plays a crucial role in enforcing SOD within DevOps environments. Many DevOps tools, such as Kubernetes, Docker, Terraform, and Ansible, require elevated privileges to manage infrastructure and deployments. Without strict access controls, DevOps engineers may inadvertently or intentionally gain excessive privileges that violate SOD policies. Organizations should implement just-in-time (JIT) privileged access, granting temporary elevated permissions only when needed and revoking them automatically once the task is completed. Additionally, all privileged sessions should be monitored, logged, and subject to audit reviews to ensure accountability and compliance with SOD policies.

Infrastructure-as-Code (IaC) and Configuration-as-Code (CaC) are integral to DevOps but also present risks when SOD is not enforced. Engineers use IaC tools such as Terraform, AWS CloudFormation, and Azure Resource Manager to define and deploy cloud infrastructure automatically. If a single individual has permission to write, approve, and execute these scripts, there is no independent validation, increasing the risk of misconfigurations, data exposure, or intentional backdoors. Organizations should implement policy-as-code solutions to enforce SOD at the infrastructure level. These solutions automatically validate configurations against security policies before allowing changes to be deployed. By integrating automated security and compliance checks into the DevOps pipeline, organizations can prevent unauthorized infrastructure modifications.

DevSecOps integrates security into DevOps workflows and is essential for maintaining SOD compliance. Traditional security reviews often slow down Agile and DevOps processes, leading to resistance from development teams. DevSecOps addresses this challenge by embedding security controls directly into CI/CD pipelines. Automated security testing tools can analyze code for vulnerabilities, verify access control configurations, and enforce compliance policies without disrupting development velocity. Security gates can be configured to block deployments if SOD violations are detected, ensuring that unauthorized code or configuration changes do not reach production environments. By treating security as code, organizations can enforce SOD dynamically without hindering Agile development practices.

GitOps, an extension of DevOps, introduces additional SOD considerations by using Git repositories as the single source of truth for infrastructure and application configurations. In a GitOps model, all changes to infrastructure and application deployments are managed through pull requests and version-controlled repositories. This approach inherently supports SOD by requiring peer reviews before changes are merged into production. However, organizations must enforce strict repository access controls to prevent unauthorized modifications. Branch protection rules, multi-person approvals, and audit logs should be implemented to ensure that no single individual can make changes without oversight. By leveraging GitOps principles, organizations can enhance SOD enforcement while maintaining agility in deployment processes.

Cloud-native environments further complicate SOD enforcement due to the decentralized nature of cloud services. Developers and DevOps teams often require access to cloud resources, containers, and serverless applications, making it challenging to implement traditional SOD controls. Cloud Identity and Access Management (Cloud IAM) solutions help enforce SOD by defining fine-grained access policies that restrict privileges based on job roles, responsibilities, and contextual attributes. Attribute-Based Access Control (ABAC) allows organizations to apply dynamic SOD policies that consider factors such as time, location, and risk level before granting access. Automated access reviews ensure that developers do not retain excessive privileges over time, reducing the risk of privilege escalation and security breaches.

SOD compliance in DevOps and Agile environments must also align with regulatory requirements. Many industries are subject to stringent compliance standards such as the General Data Protection Regulation (GDPR), Sarbanes-Oxley Act (SOX), and Payment Card Industry Data Security Standard (PCI DSS), which require strict access controls and audit trails. Organizations must document their SOD policies, maintain access logs, and conduct periodic audits to demonstrate compliance. Automated compliance reporting tools provide visibility into access controls, privileged user activities, and policy enforcement, helping organizations meet regulatory obligations without slowing down development cycles.

Training and awareness programs are essential for ensuring that DevOps teams understand SOD principles and their importance in security and compliance. Developers and engineers often view security controls as obstacles to efficiency, leading to resistance when SOD policies are enforced. Organizations must educate teams on best practices for secure coding, access management, and privilege separation. Security champions can be embedded within DevOps teams to promote security awareness and ensure that SOD policies are integrated seamlessly into development workflows. By fostering a culture of security, organizations can align DevOps agility with SOD compliance without creating unnecessary friction.

As DevOps and Agile methodologies continue to evolve, organizations must adopt adaptive SOD enforcement strategies that balance security, compliance, and operational efficiency. By implementing RBAC and ABAC, securing CI/CD pipelines, integrating DevSecOps, enforcing GitOps best practices, leveraging cloud IAM solutions, and automating compliance monitoring, organizations can maintain strong SOD controls without hindering development speed. A proactive approach to SOD in DevOps environments ensures that security and compliance are maintained without compromising the agility and innovation that DevOps aims to achieve.

SOD in Financial and Banking Sectors

Segregation of Duties (SOD) is a critical security and compliance measure in the financial and banking sectors, ensuring that no single individual has unchecked control over financial transactions, account management, loan approvals, or regulatory reporting. The financial industry is highly regulated, with stringent requirements for internal controls to prevent fraud, unauthorized transactions, money laundering, and financial misstatements. Without proper SOD enforcement, banks and financial institutions expose themselves to significant risks, including operational fraud, insider threats, regulatory fines, and reputational damage. Implementing strong SOD policies within financial operations is essential for maintaining trust, securing sensitive financial assets, and ensuring compliance with industry regulations.

One of the primary areas where SOD is enforced in the financial sector is transaction processing. Banks and financial institutions handle billions of transactions daily, including deposits, withdrawals, wire transfers, loan disbursements, and payments. To prevent fraudulent activities, SOD policies require that different employees handle different stages of a transaction. For example, the individual who initiates a wire transfer request should not be the same person who approves and executes it. Additionally, reconciliation of transactions must be conducted by an independent party to ensure that all financial records match without manipulation. By implementing these controls, financial institutions reduce the risk of unauthorized transactions and misappropriation of funds.

Loan approvals and credit management also require strict SOD enforcement. Lending decisions involve multiple steps, including application review, credit risk assessment, approval, and fund disbursement. If a single employee has authority over all these processes, there is a high risk of biased decision-making, fraudulent approvals, or personal gain. To mitigate these risks, banks enforce SOD policies that separate loan origination, underwriting, and disbursement functions. Underwriters assess creditworthiness based on financial data, while loan officers review applications and ensure compliance with lending policies. Final approval is granted by senior management or an independent credit committee, ensuring that no single individual has full control over loan issuance.

In financial reporting and accounting, SOD plays a crucial role in preventing financial misstatements, fraud, and regulatory violations. Financial institutions must comply with strict accounting standards, such as Generally Accepted Accounting Principles (GAAP) and International Financial Reporting Standards (IFRS). SOD policies ensure that employees responsible for recording financial transactions are separate from those who prepare financial statements and those who conduct audits. This separation prevents manipulation of financial data and ensures accurate reporting to regulators, shareholders, and stakeholders. Internal audit teams play a key role in enforcing SOD by conducting independent reviews of financial statements, identifying discrepancies, and ensuring compliance with accounting principles.

Regulatory compliance is a major driver of SOD enforcement in the financial and banking sectors. Regulations such as the Sarbanes-Oxley Act (SOX), Basel III, the Dodd-Frank Act, and the Payment Card Industry Data Security Standard (PCI DSS) mandate strict internal controls, risk assessments, and audit trails. These regulations require financial institutions to implement access control measures that prevent conflicts of interest, unauthorized transactions, and data breaches. Regulatory audits often focus on whether SOD policies are effectively enforced, requiring banks to maintain detailed logs of user activities, role assignments, and transaction approvals. Failure to comply with these regulations can result in severe penalties, including multimillion-dollar fines, legal liabilities, and loss of operating licenses.

Fraud prevention is another critical aspect of SOD enforcement in financial institutions. Insider fraud, where employees exploit their positions for personal gain, is a significant risk in banking operations. Common fraud schemes include embezzlement, unauthorized account modifications, loan fraud, and falsified transactions. SOD policies prevent fraud by ensuring that key financial processes require multiple levels of authorization. For example, bank tellers processing cash withdrawals above a certain limit must obtain approval from a supervisor before completing the transaction. Similarly, financial analysts reviewing investment portfolios must be separate from those executing trades to prevent market manipulation or conflicts of interest. By enforcing SOD, banks create an environment of checks and balances that reduces the likelihood of fraudulent activities.

Privileged access management (PAM) is an essential component of SOD enforcement in banking IT systems. Financial institutions rely on core banking platforms, payment gateways, customer relationship management (CRM) systems, and financial reporting tools to conduct operations. If privileged users, such as database administrators or IT security personnel, have unrestricted access to these systems, they could manipulate transaction records, alter account balances, or bypass security controls. PAM solutions enforce SOD by restricting privileged access, requiring multi-factor authentication (MFA), and implementing just-in-time (JIT) access provisioning. All privileged user activities should be logged, monitored, and audited to detect unauthorized modifications and ensure compliance with security policies.

Identity and Access Management (IAM) solutions play a crucial role in automating SOD enforcement within financial institutions. These systems integrate with banking applications to define role-based access controls (RBAC), preventing employees from accumulating conflicting privileges. IAM tools continuously analyze user access, detect violations, and enforce corrective actions, such as revoking unnecessary permissions or requiring additional approvals. Machine learning-driven IAM solutions enhance SOD compliance by identifying unusual access patterns, predicting potential fraud risks, and triggering automated alerts when policy violations occur. By leveraging IAM technology, banks and financial institutions can enforce SOD policies consistently across all departments and operational workflows.

Third-party risk management is another critical area where SOD must be enforced. Banks frequently engage external vendors, consultants, and contractors who require access to financial systems, customer data, and regulatory reporting tools. Without strict SOD policies, third-party users may obtain excessive privileges, increasing the risk of data breaches or regulatory violations. Financial institutions must enforce least privilege access for external users, ensuring that they can only perform approved actions within the scope of their responsibilities. Vendor access should be time-restricted, continuously monitored, and subject to periodic reviews to ensure compliance with security policies and contractual agreements.

Monitoring and auditing are essential for maintaining SOD compliance in the financial sector. Continuous monitoring tools track user activities, transaction approvals, and system modifications in real-time, enabling security teams to detect anomalies and investigate suspicious behavior. Security Information and Event Management (SIEM) solutions aggregate log data from multiple banking systems, providing visibility into access control violations, unauthorized transactions, and fraudulent activities. Regular SOD audits help identify policy gaps, assess compliance with regulatory requirements, and refine internal controls. Financial institutions must conduct periodic reviews of SOD policies, ensuring that they remain effective in mitigating evolving threats and regulatory changes.

Employee training and awareness programs support SOD enforcement by educating banking personnel on access control policies, fraud prevention strategies, and regulatory compliance requirements. Many financial fraud cases occur due to insider threats, negligence, or lack of awareness regarding security best practices. Banks should provide regular training sessions to ensure that employees understand their role in maintaining SOD compliance, recognizing security risks, and reporting suspicious activities. Security awareness initiatives create a culture of accountability and reinforce the importance of adhering to SOD policies in daily banking operations.

As financial institutions continue to embrace digital transformation, online banking, and fintech integrations, SOD enforcement must evolve to address emerging security risks. By implementing RBAC and PAM controls, automating IAM policies, continuously monitoring financial transactions, and aligning with regulatory compliance requirements, banks can maintain strong SOD enforcement while enabling secure and efficient financial operations. A robust SOD framework ensures the integrity of banking transactions, protects customer assets, and upholds trust in the financial sector.

SOD in Healthcare and Pharmaceuticals

Segregation of Duties (SOD) is a crucial element in healthcare and pharmaceutical industries, where regulatory compliance, patient safety, data security, and financial integrity are top priorities. These industries handle sensitive patient records, prescription data, clinical trials, drug manufacturing processes, and financial transactions, all of which require strict access control and operational oversight. Without proper SOD enforcement, healthcare institutions and pharmaceutical companies expose themselves to risks such as fraud, data breaches, medical errors, regulatory penalties, and compromised patient safety. Implementing strong SOD policies ensures that key tasks are divided among multiple individuals, preventing conflicts of interest and unauthorized actions while maintaining compliance with industry regulations.

One of the most critical areas where SOD must be enforced in healthcare is electronic health records (EHR) management. Healthcare providers store and process vast amounts of protected health information (PHI), including patient histories, prescriptions, diagnostic reports, and billing records. To prevent unauthorized access and data tampering, SOD policies ensure that no single individual has unrestricted control over patient records. For example, a physician should have access to modify patient treatment plans but should not be able to alter billing information, while administrative staff managing billing should not have access to modify medical records. Role-based access control (RBAC) in EHR systems helps enforce these policies, ensuring that each healthcare worker can only access the data necessary for their job function.

Pharmaceutical research and clinical trials require strict SOD enforcement to maintain the integrity of drug development processes and regulatory compliance. Clinical trials involve multiple phases, including study design, data collection, analysis, and regulatory submission. If a single researcher has full control over data entry and results analysis, the risk of data manipulation or bias increases. SOD policies ensure that different teams handle data collection, statistical analysis, and regulatory reporting independently. Research institutions and pharmaceutical companies must implement role separation to prevent conflicts of interest and ensure the accuracy and credibility of clinical trial data. Audit trails and automated monitoring help detect unauthorized changes and maintain compliance with regulatory bodies such as the Food and Drug Administration (FDA) and the European Medicines Agency (EMA).

Manufacturing and supply chain operations in the pharmaceutical industry also require robust SOD controls. The drug manufacturing process involves multiple stages, including raw material procurement, formulation, quality control, packaging, and distribution. SOD policies ensure that individuals responsible for procuring raw materials do not have authority over quality control approvals, preventing fraudulent practices such as substituting inferior ingredients. Similarly, employees involved in drug formulation should not have the ability to modify manufacturing logs or approve final product shipments. Implementing SOD in pharmaceutical manufacturing helps prevent counterfeiting, ensures compliance with Good Manufacturing Practices (GMP), and protects consumers from defective or unsafe medications.

Regulatory compliance is a major driver of SOD enforcement in healthcare and pharmaceuticals. Organizations in these industries must comply with strict regulatory frameworks such as the Health Insurance Portability and Accountability Act (HIPAA), FDA 21 CFR Part 11, the Drug Supply Chain Security Act (DSCSA), and the General Data Protection Regulation (GDPR). These regulations require organizations to implement access controls, maintain audit trails, and enforce data integrity measures to prevent unauthorized access, fraud, and medical errors. Regulatory auditors often scrutinize SOD policies to ensure that sensitive medical data and drug manufacturing processes are properly secured. Failure to comply with these regulations can result in legal penalties, loss of operating licenses, and reputational damage.

Pharmaceutical financial operations also require SOD enforcement to prevent fraud and accounting misstatements. Large pharmaceutical companies handle billions of dollars in revenue from drug sales, research grants, and government contracts. Without proper access segregation, financial fraud, misappropriation of funds, or improper financial reporting could go undetected. Organizations must ensure that employees involved in processing payments, managing supplier contracts, and reconciling financial transactions do not have conflicting privileges. For example, an employee responsible for approving invoices should not have the ability to modify supplier bank details or process payments. Implementing automated access controls and regular financial audits helps enforce SOD policies and ensures compliance with the Sarbanes-Oxley Act (SOX) and other financial regulations.

Identity and Access Management (IAM) solutions play a key role in automating SOD enforcement in healthcare and pharmaceutical organizations. IAM platforms provide centralized access control, allowing organizations to define user roles, enforce least privilege access, and detect SOD conflicts across multiple applications. Automated IAM solutions continuously monitor user access rights, detect policy violations, and generate reports for compliance audits. Integration with Security Information and Event Management (SIEM) systems further enhances security by correlating access events with potential threats, enabling organizations to respond to suspicious activities in real-time.

Privileged Access Management (PAM) is another critical component of SOD enforcement in healthcare IT and pharmaceutical research environments. Privileged users, such as database administrators, IT security personnel, and research scientists, often require elevated permissions to access critical systems. Without proper governance, these users could bypass security controls, modify sensitive data, or introduce vulnerabilities. PAM solutions enforce just-in-time (JIT) access provisioning, ensuring that privileged access is granted only when necessary and for a limited duration. All privileged activities should be logged and monitored to prevent unauthorized modifications and ensure compliance with SOD policies.

Supply chain security in the pharmaceutical industry requires continuous SOD monitoring to prevent counterfeit drugs from entering the market. Pharmaceutical companies must track the movement of drugs from manufacturing plants to wholesalers, pharmacies, and healthcare providers. Blockchain technology is increasingly being used to enforce SOD policies in supply chain management, ensuring transparency and traceability of pharmaceutical products. By implementing decentralized ledger systems, organizations can verify the authenticity of drugs, prevent fraudulent transactions, and ensure compliance with global drug safety regulations.

Third-party risk management is another key aspect of SOD enforcement in healthcare and pharmaceuticals. These industries rely on external vendors, research collaborators, and contract manufacturers who require access to sensitive data and systems. Without strict SOD policies, third-party users may gain excessive privileges, increasing the risk of data breaches and regulatory non-compliance. Organizations must enforce least privilege access for third-party vendors, ensuring that they can only perform approved actions within the scope of their contractual obligations. Vendor access should be time-limited, continuously monitored, and subject to periodic reviews to prevent unauthorized activities.

Employee training and awareness programs support SOD compliance by educating healthcare and pharmaceutical staff on access control best practices, data security, and regulatory requirements. Many security breaches occur due to insider threats or accidental policy violations caused by a lack of awareness. Organizations should provide regular training sessions to ensure that employees understand their responsibilities in maintaining SOD compliance, recognizing security risks, and reporting suspicious activities. Security awareness initiatives create a culture of accountability and reinforce the importance of adhering to SOD policies in daily operations.

As healthcare and pharmaceutical industries continue to adopt digital transformation initiatives, including cloud-based EHR systems, AI-driven drug discovery, and automated manufacturing, SOD enforcement must evolve to address emerging security risks. By implementing IAM and PAM controls, securing supply chain processes, automating access reviews, and aligning with regulatory compliance requirements, organizations can maintain strong SOD enforcement while improving efficiency and innovation. A comprehensive SOD framework ensures the integrity of patient data, protects pharmaceutical research, and upholds trust in healthcare and drug development industries.

SOD in Government and Public Sector Organizations

Segregation of Duties (SOD) is a fundamental principle in government and public sector organizations, ensuring transparency, accountability, and compliance with regulations. Government institutions are responsible for managing public funds, administering social programs, enforcing laws, and maintaining critical infrastructure. These responsibilities require strict access controls and separation of duties to prevent fraud, corruption, mismanagement, and unauthorized access to sensitive data. Without effective SOD enforcement, government agencies risk financial losses, security breaches, and a loss of public trust. Implementing strong SOD policies within government operations ensures that key tasks are divided among multiple individuals, reducing the risk of conflicts of interest and unauthorized actions while maintaining operational integrity.

Public financial management is one of the most critical areas where SOD must be enforced. Government agencies handle large-scale financial transactions, including budget allocations, procurement contracts, tax collections, and public benefits disbursements. SOD policies prevent a single employee from having complete control over financial processes, reducing the risk of embezzlement or fraudulent transactions. For example, an official responsible for approving vendor contracts should not have the authority to authorize payments to those vendors. Similarly, auditors reviewing government expenditures must remain independent from those responsible for budget planning and financial reporting. By implementing these controls, government institutions can prevent financial mismanagement and ensure compliance with financial regulations such as the Government Accountability Office (GAO) standards and the International Public Sector Accounting Standards (IPSAS).

Procurement and contract management in government institutions require strict SOD enforcement to prevent conflicts of interest, favoritism, and fraud. Government agencies regularly procure goods and services for infrastructure projects, defense contracts, public health initiatives, and technology upgrades. If procurement officers have unchecked control over contract selection and approval, they may engage in unethical practices such as bid-rigging or preferential treatment of vendors. SOD policies require that different personnel oversee procurement planning, contract evaluation, approval, and financial disbursement. Independent review committees, compliance officers, and audit teams must be involved in contract oversight to ensure fair competition and transparency. Digital procurement platforms integrated with automated SOD enforcement mechanisms further enhance accountability by tracking every stage of the procurement process.

Tax administration and revenue collection are another critical area where SOD plays a vital role in preventing fraud and ensuring compliance. Tax authorities handle sensitive financial information, process payments, and enforce tax regulations. If a single employee has the authority to modify tax records, approve refunds, and process payments, there is a high risk of fraud and manipulation. SOD policies ensure that tax assessment, collection, and auditing functions are handled by separate teams, preventing any individual from exploiting the system. Automated tax systems with built-in SOD controls help detect unauthorized modifications, flag suspicious transactions, and enforce access restrictions based on predefined roles and responsibilities.

Law enforcement and national security agencies must enforce SOD to maintain operational integrity and prevent abuses of power. Government security agencies, police departments, and intelligence services handle classified data, conduct investigations, and enforce laws. If access to case files, surveillance data, and operational plans is not properly segregated, there is a risk of unauthorized leaks, corruption, or misuse of power. SOD policies ensure that law enforcement officers, analysts, and oversight committees operate independently, preventing conflicts of interest and unauthorized access to sensitive information. Identity and Access Management (IAM) solutions help enforce these policies by defining role-based access controls (RBAC), restricting access to classified information, and continuously monitoring user activity for security violations.

Public sector cybersecurity and IT governance require robust SOD enforcement to protect critical government systems from cyber threats and insider risks. Government IT departments manage sensitive citizen data, national security information, and digital services. Without proper SOD policies, privileged users such as system administrators, database managers, and IT security personnel could exploit their access for unauthorized activities. Privileged Access Management (PAM) solutions enforce least privilege access, ensuring that administrative privileges are granted only when necessary and for a limited duration. Continuous monitoring and audit logs provide transparency into system modifications, preventing unauthorized changes that could compromise national security or public trust.

Regulatory compliance is a significant driver of SOD enforcement in government agencies. Many government institutions must comply with regulations such as the Federal Information Security Management Act (FISMA), the European Union's General Data Protection Regulation (GDPR), and national anti-corruption laws. These regulations require government agencies to implement strict access controls, conduct periodic audits, and maintain accountability in public sector operations. SOD policies help agencies comply with these regulations by ensuring that financial transactions, personnel decisions, and data access are properly segregated and reviewed. Compliance automation tools help government agencies generate audit reports, track policy violations, and ensure alignment with legal mandates.

Public health and social services programs rely on SOD to prevent fraud and ensure equitable distribution of benefits. Government agencies manage healthcare programs, unemployment benefits, and social welfare initiatives that serve millions of citizens. Without proper SOD enforcement, fraudulent claims, misallocation of resources, and corruption could undermine the effectiveness of these programs. SOD policies ensure that eligibility assessments, benefit approvals, and financial disbursements are handled by different departments, reducing the risk of conflicts of interest. Automated case management systems with integrated SOD controls help prevent unauthorized modifications to beneficiary records and ensure fair and transparent program administration.

Human resource management in government institutions also requires SOD enforcement to prevent favoritism, unauthorized hiring, and payroll fraud. Public sector HR departments oversee hiring, promotions, salary payments, and employee benefits. Without SOD controls, HR personnel could manipulate payroll records, approve unauthorized salary increases, or grant benefits to ineligible employees. SOD policies ensure that different personnel oversee hiring decisions, payroll processing, and benefits approval, preventing unauthorized modifications to employee records. Automated HR systems with access control mechanisms provide transparency and accountability in personnel management, reducing the risk of fraudulent activities.

Citizen data privacy and access governance are critical concerns for government agencies handling sensitive personal information. Government institutions collect and store vast amounts of citizen data, including identification records, healthcare information, financial data, and legal documents. Without proper SOD enforcement, unauthorized access or data breaches could compromise privacy and national security. SOD policies ensure that data collection, storage, processing, and sharing are handled by separate entities with appropriate oversight. Role-based access controls (RBAC), encryption, and data masking technologies further enhance security by limiting access to sensitive information based on job responsibilities. Continuous monitoring and data access audits help detect and prevent unauthorized data access.

Public sector transparency and anti-corruption initiatives rely on SOD to maintain integrity in government operations. Government institutions are accountable to the public, requiring strict internal controls to prevent corruption, abuse of power, and financial mismanagement. SOD policies help establish clear lines of responsibility, ensuring that decision-making processes are transparent and subject to oversight. Whistleblower protection programs and anonymous reporting mechanisms further strengthen SOD enforcement by allowing employees to report potential policy violations without fear of retaliation. By integrating SOD with anti-corruption frameworks, government agencies can reinforce public trust and demonstrate commitment to ethical governance.

As government and public sector organizations continue to modernize, adopting digital services, cloud computing, and AI-driven automation, SOD enforcement must evolve to address new security challenges. Implementing IAM and PAM controls, automating compliance monitoring, integrating AI-driven risk analysis, and ensuring role-based access controls help maintain strong SOD policies across all government functions. A comprehensive SOD framework safeguards public funds, protects citizen data, and ensures the integrity and transparency of government operations.

SOD in Manufacturing and Supply Chain Security

Segregation of Duties (SOD) plays a crucial role in manufacturing and supply chain security, ensuring that no single individual has excessive control over critical processes, financial transactions, procurement, inventory management, and quality control. The manufacturing industry is highly dependent on complex supply chains that involve multiple stakeholders, including suppliers, logistics providers, production teams, and distribution networks. Without proper SOD enforcement, organizations expose themselves to risks such as fraud, theft, supply chain disruptions, counterfeit materials, regulatory violations, and operational inefficiencies. Implementing SOD policies in manufacturing and supply chain security helps maintain accountability, prevent conflicts of interest, and ensure compliance with industry regulations.

One of the most critical areas where SOD must be enforced is procurement and supplier management. Manufacturing companies rely on suppliers for raw materials, components, and equipment necessary for production. If procurement officers have unchecked control over supplier selection, contract negotiations, and payment approvals, there is a significant risk of fraud, bribery, and conflicts of interest. SOD policies require that different individuals handle supplier evaluation, purchase order approvals, and payment processing. For example, the employee responsible for selecting a supplier should not have the authority to approve invoices and payments to that supplier.

Independent review teams or automated procurement platforms with built-in SOD controls help prevent unauthorized transactions and ensure transparency in supplier relationships.

Inventory management and warehouse operations also require strict SOD enforcement to prevent theft, misappropriation, and stock manipulation. Manufacturing companies store large quantities of raw materials and finished goods in warehouses and distribution centers. If the same individual is responsible for inventory tracking, stock movement approvals, and financial reconciliation, there is a high risk of inventory fraud. SOD policies ensure that inventory audits are conducted by personnel independent of those managing stock movements. Automated warehouse management systems with role-based access controls (RBAC) further enhance security by restricting inventory access based on job functions. Real-time monitoring and audit logs help detect discrepancies, ensuring that inventory records match actual stock levels.

Production and quality control processes require separation of duties to maintain product integrity and compliance with industry standards. Manufacturing companies must adhere to strict quality assurance protocols to ensure that products meet safety, performance, and regulatory requirements. If employees responsible for production also oversee quality inspections, there is a risk of compromised quality control and falsified testing results. SOD policies require that production teams, quality control personnel, and compliance officers operate independently. Automated quality management systems (QMS) enforce SOD by ensuring that inspection approvals are handled by authorized quality control teams rather than production staff. Independent audits and regulatory inspections further strengthen quality assurance, preventing defective or non-compliant products from reaching the market.

Supply chain security is another critical aspect of SOD enforcement, particularly in industries with global supply networks. Manufacturing companies rely on third-party logistics providers, transportation companies, and customs agencies to move raw materials and finished products across international borders. If supply chain managers have control over vendor selection, shipment approvals, and financial transactions, there is a risk of fraudulent shipping practices, smuggling, or unauthorized diversions. SOD policies ensure that logistics coordinators, compliance teams, and finance departments operate independently, preventing unauthorized modifications to shipping documents or payment approvals. Blockchain technology is increasingly being used to enhance supply chain transparency, allowing organizations to track and verify every step of the supply chain with immutable audit logs.

Cybersecurity in manufacturing and supply chain operations requires robust SOD enforcement to prevent insider threats, data breaches, and unauthorized access to critical systems. Manufacturing companies rely on industrial control systems (ICS), enterprise resource planning (ERP) platforms, and supply chain management software to manage production, logistics, and inventory. If IT administrators have unrestricted access to modify system configurations, user permissions, and financial transactions, there is a high risk of security breaches. Privileged Access Management (PAM) solutions enforce least privilege access, ensuring that IT personnel receive temporary, role-based permissions rather than permanent administrative control. Multi-factor authentication (MFA), continuous monitoring, and automated alerts help detect unauthorized access attempts, mitigating cybersecurity risks.

Compliance with industry regulations and trade laws is another major reason for enforcing SOD in manufacturing and supply chain security. Regulations such as the International Traffic in Arms Regulations (ITAR), the General Data Protection Regulation (GDPR), and the Customs-Trade Partnership Against Terrorism (C-TPAT) require manufacturing companies to implement strict access controls, document supply chain activities, and prevent unauthorized modifications to trade records. Regulatory audits often focus on whether SOD policies are properly enforced, requiring companies to maintain detailed logs of procurement decisions, inventory transactions, and supply chain modifications. Automated compliance tracking tools help organizations ensure that SOD policies align with legal requirements, reducing the risk of regulatory fines and trade restrictions.

Counterfeit prevention in supply chain operations is another critical function of SOD enforcement. The presence of counterfeit materials, unauthorized substitutions, or unverified suppliers can compromise product safety and brand reputation. Manufacturing companies must implement SOD policies that separate supplier approval, material inspection, and procurement functions to prevent counterfeit products from entering the supply chain. Advanced authentication technologies such as RFID tracking, serial number verification, and AI-driven supply chain analytics help organizations detect fraudulent materials before they reach production lines. Independent testing laboratories and third-party verification agencies further enhance counterfeit prevention efforts by providing objective assessments of material authenticity.

Automated SOD enforcement through IAM and ERP systems helps manufacturing companies maintain security and operational efficiency. Enterprise IAM solutions integrate with manufacturing systems to define access controls, detect unauthorized transactions, and enforce approval workflows. AI-driven analytics enhance SOD monitoring by identifying unusual access patterns, predicting supply chain risks, and triggering alerts when policy violations occur. By integrating IAM with supply chain management platforms, organizations can enforce SOD policies dynamically, ensuring that only authorized personnel have access to sensitive manufacturing and logistics data.

Third-party risk management is another key aspect of SOD enforcement in supply chain security. Manufacturing companies often collaborate with external suppliers, logistics providers, and contractors who require access to proprietary designs, production facilities, and distribution networks. Without strict SOD policies, third-party users may gain excessive privileges, increasing the risk of intellectual property theft, supply chain disruptions, or regulatory non-compliance. Organizations must implement least privilege access controls for external partners, ensuring that they can only perform approved actions within their assigned scope. Time-restricted access, continuous monitoring, and periodic third-party audits help prevent unauthorized activities and protect manufacturing assets.

Employee training and awareness programs play a critical role in supporting SOD compliance in manufacturing and supply chain security. Many operational risks arise from human error, negligence, or lack of awareness regarding security best practices. Organizations should provide regular training sessions on fraud prevention, inventory security, procurement ethics, and access management. Employees must understand their responsibilities in enforcing SOD policies and recognize potential risks associated with unauthorized access, financial fraud, and counterfeit materials. A strong culture of security awareness ensures that SOD policies are actively followed and integrated into daily manufacturing and supply chain operations.

As manufacturing and supply chain operations continue to evolve with digital transformation, automation, and global trade complexities, SOD enforcement must adapt to emerging security challenges. By implementing IAM and PAM solutions, securing procurement and logistics operations, preventing counterfeit risks, automating compliance tracking, and strengthening cybersecurity measures, organizations can maintain robust SOD enforcement while optimizing operational efficiency. A well-defined SOD framework enhances supply chain integrity, protects manufacturing assets, and ensures compliance with global trade and industry regulations.

Case Studies: Successful SOD Implementations

Segregation of Duties (SOD) is a fundamental security and compliance principle that ensures accountability, transparency, and fraud prevention in various industries. Organizations that have successfully implemented SOD policies have significantly reduced the risk of insider threats, financial fraud, and regulatory violations while improving operational efficiency. The following case studies highlight real-world examples of effective SOD enforcement across different sectors, demonstrating how organizations have leveraged technology, automation, and governance frameworks to strengthen security and compliance.

A global financial institution faced increasing regulatory scrutiny regarding internal controls and fraud prevention. The organization had a complex IT infrastructure with thousands of employees accessing financial systems for transaction processing, loan approvals, and investment management. The lack of proper SOD enforcement led to cases where individuals had both initiation and approval rights over high-value transactions, increasing the risk of unauthorized fund transfers. To address these challenges, the institution implemented a robust IAM solution integrated with a role-based access control (RBAC) model. By redefining user roles, implementing multi-tier approval workflows, and automating access reviews, the bank significantly reduced instances of privilege accumulation and unauthorized financial transactions. Continuous monitoring tools flagged access anomalies, ensuring that violations were detected in real-time. As a result, the financial institution improved compliance with Sarbanes-Oxley (SOX) regulations, strengthened fraud prevention, and enhanced overall operational transparency.

A multinational pharmaceutical company needed to improve compliance with FDA regulations governing clinical trials and drug manufacturing. Previously, researchers had access to modify both data collection and analysis processes, leading to potential risks of data manipulation. Additionally, laboratory staff could approve their own quality control tests, compromising the integrity of drug safety procedures. The company implemented SOD policies by restructuring job roles and implementing an Attribute-Based Access Control (ABAC) model. Laboratory staff were restricted from approving their own test results, and researchers were assigned read-only access to clinical trial data. Automated access logs and audit trails ensured that any attempt to bypass these controls triggered alerts for security teams. These measures not only strengthened regulatory compliance but also improved the reliability of clinical data, leading to faster drug approvals and enhanced patient safety.

A government tax agency encountered security breaches due to unauthorized modifications of taxpayer records. Certain employees had excessive access privileges, allowing them to alter tax liabilities and process fraudulent refunds without oversight. The agency adopted a Privileged Access Management (PAM) solution to enforce SOD policies, ensuring that employees handling tax assessments could not process refunds independently. Time-limited access was granted for high-risk transactions, requiring multiple approvals before any tax modifications could be finalized. Additionally, all privileged activities were recorded and reviewed by an independent audit team. These enhancements eliminated fraudulent transactions, increased transparency, and ensured compliance with financial regulations. The successful implementation of SOD policies restored public confidence in the tax agency's operations and improved overall revenue collection integrity.

A leading global manufacturing company faced inventory fraud and financial losses due to weak access controls in its supply chain operations. Warehouse managers had the ability to both approve inventory orders and modify stock records, leading to cases of missing inventory and unauthorized shipments. To mitigate these risks, the company enforced strict SOD policies by integrating access control measures into its Enterprise Resource Planning (ERP) system. Warehouse managers were restricted from modifying stock levels after approving shipments, while a separate team handled inventory reconciliation. Blockchain technology was introduced to track the movement of raw materials and finished goods, creating an immutable record of all supply chain transactions. This new SOD framework significantly reduced inventory discrepancies, prevented fraudulent stock modifications, and improved supplier accountability.

An international retail company experienced repeated cybersecurity incidents due to inadequate access controls in its IT environment. IT administrators had unrestricted privileges across the company's cloud and on-premises infrastructure, allowing unauthorized changes to critical systems. After a security audit revealed multiple SOD violations, the company implemented an Identity Governance and Administration (IGA) solution. Access requests for administrative privileges were subjected to approval workflows, requiring multi-factor authentication and just-in-time (JIT) access provisioning. Real-time session monitoring and logging ensured that all privileged actions were recorded for audit purposes. This SOD enforcement strategy reduced the risk of insider threats, improved cybersecurity resilience, and ensured compliance with GDPR and PCI DSS regulations.

A healthcare provider needed to secure electronic health records (EHR) while maintaining efficient patient care workflows. Doctors, nurses, and administrative staff required different levels of access to patient records, but improper role assignments led to unauthorized access incidents. To enforce SOD, the healthcare provider implemented role-based access controls, ensuring that administrative staff could view billing information but could not modify patient diagnoses or prescriptions. Multi-tiered access approvals were introduced for modifying critical patient data, preventing unauthorized alterations to medical records. Automated audit logs tracked every access attempt, enabling quick detection of policy violations. These SOD enhancements safeguarded patient privacy, strengthened compliance with HIPAA regulations, and improved trust in the healthcare provider's data security practices.

A Fortune 500 energy company faced compliance challenges due to improper access management in its operational technology (OT) environment. Engineers managing power grid systems had excessive privileges, allowing them to override safety mechanisms without oversight. To address this risk, the company enforced SOD policies by implementing a zero-trust architecture combined with continuous monitoring solutions. Engineers were restricted from executing critical control commands without independent verification from a second team. AI-powered anomaly detection tools identified any deviations from normal operational behavior, preventing unauthorized changes to energy infrastructure. This SOD enforcement approach significantly reduced the risk of cyber-physical attacks, improved compliance with energy sector regulations, and enhanced overall system reliability.

A large logistics company needed to strengthen SOD policies in its freight tracking and customs operations. Employees responsible for approving shipments had the ability to modify customs documentation, leading to smuggling risks and regulatory violations. The company integrated automated document validation systems with blockchain-based supply chain tracking to ensure that shipment approvals and customs modifications were handled by different teams. Role-based access controls ensured that employees could only perform tasks aligned with their job responsibilities. Any attempt to alter shipment records triggered alerts for security teams. This new framework improved customs compliance, reduced cargo theft, and increased the efficiency of international trade operations.

An insurance company faced fraudulent claims due to SOD violations in its claims processing system. Claims adjusters could approve their own claims, leading to unauthorized payouts and financial losses. To enforce SOD, the company implemented an automated claims verification system that required separate approvals from different departments. Machine learning-based fraud detection tools analyzed claim patterns and flagged suspicious transactions for manual review. These SOD enhancements significantly reduced fraudulent payouts, strengthened compliance with industry regulations, and improved customer trust in the claims process.

These successful SOD implementations demonstrate the importance of access control frameworks in protecting financial assets, securing sensitive data, and ensuring regulatory compliance. By leveraging IAM, PAM, ABAC, IGA, blockchain, and AI-driven security tools, organizations across various industries have effectively mitigated risks, improved operational efficiency, and maintained compliance with global regulations. The lessons learned from these case studies highlight the necessity of continuously refining SOD policies, integrating automated monitoring solutions, and fostering a culture of accountability to sustain long-term security and compliance.

Case Studies: Failures in SOD and Lessons Learned

Segregation of Duties (SOD) is a fundamental security principle that prevents fraud, operational inefficiencies, and regulatory violations. However, many organizations fail to enforce SOD effectively, leading to serious financial losses, security breaches, compliance failures, and reputational damage. Examining real-world failures in SOD implementation provides valuable insights into common mistakes, weaknesses in access control frameworks, and lessons learned from these incidents. These case studies highlight the risks associated with poor SOD enforcement and the importance of continuous monitoring, automation, and governance in mitigating these risks.

A major financial institution suffered a multi-million-dollar fraud scandal due to weak SOD controls in its payment processing system. The bank allowed employees in its accounts payable department to both create and approve vendor payments without independent verification. Over time, an employee exploited this lack of oversight by creating fake vendor accounts and approving fraudulent payments to personal bank accounts. The fraud remained undetected for years because access reviews were performed infrequently, and audit logs were not actively monitored. When the fraud was finally uncovered, the financial institution faced regulatory fines, legal consequences, and severe reputational damage. The primary lesson learned from this failure was the necessity of implementing multi-tier approval workflows, automating access reviews, and enforcing stricter monitoring of financial transactions.

A global pharmaceutical company faced regulatory penalties after it was discovered that clinical trial data had been manipulated to support drug approvals. Investigations revealed that researchers had excessive privileges, allowing them to modify both raw data and final analysis reports without independent oversight. The lack of proper SOD enforcement meant that quality assurance teams did not have separate access to verify results, enabling biased reporting of drug efficacy. The regulatory fallout led to drug recalls, loss of market trust, and financial losses due to non-compliance with FDA and European Medicines Agency regulations. To prevent future violations, the company restructured its access control policies, enforcing strict separation between data collection, statistical analysis, and regulatory reporting teams. Automated audit logs and independent review processes were implemented to ensure the integrity of clinical trial data.

A national tax authority experienced a security breach when an insider exploited inadequate SOD controls to alter taxpayer records. The agency had given certain employees unrestricted access to modify tax assessments, approve refunds, and process payments. A group of insiders collaborated to change tax records, reduce tax liabilities for selected individuals, and approve fraudulent tax refunds. The fraudulent activity went undetected for several months because audit logs were not actively reviewed, and access privileges were not periodically reassessed. After the breach was exposed, the government faced a public backlash, leading to stricter regulatory oversight of tax agencies. To mitigate future risks, the agency implemented SOD policies that restricted employees from handling both assessment and refund processing. Privileged Access Management (PAM) solutions were deployed to limit administrative access, and real-time transaction monitoring was introduced to detect suspicious modifications to taxpayer records.

A multinational retailer suffered a data breach that compromised millions of customer records due to a failure in SOD enforcement within its IT department. System administrators were granted broad privileges to manage both user accounts and security logs, allowing an insider to bypass security controls without detection. The attacker exploited these privileges to install malicious software, exfiltrate customer data, and erase log files that could have traced the activity. The breach resulted in financial penalties, lawsuits, and loss of customer trust. In response, the retailer restructured its access control framework, ensuring that no single administrator had unrestricted access to both system configurations and security monitoring tools. Role-based access control (RBAC) was enforced, and SIEM solutions were integrated to provide continuous security monitoring and anomaly detection.

A government agency responsible for public benefits distribution faced widespread fraud due to inadequate SOD controls in its case management system. Social workers who reviewed and approved benefit applications also had the ability to modify eligibility criteria and authorize payments. Several employees exploited this access to approve fraudulent claims for themselves and their associates. The fraud remained undetected until a whistleblower reported discrepancies in benefit distributions. A subsequent audit revealed that access reviews were not conducted regularly, and no independent verification process was in place to prevent unauthorized changes. To strengthen SOD enforcement, the agency implemented an automated workflow system that required separate teams for eligibility verification, approval, and payment processing. AI-driven fraud detection algorithms were integrated to flag suspicious activity, significantly reducing fraudulent claims.

A major logistics company experienced significant supply chain disruptions due to a failure in SOD implementation within its procurement department. Employees responsible for supplier selection also had control over contract approvals and payment processing, creating opportunities for favoritism and financial fraud.

Some procurement managers entered into fraudulent contracts with shell companies, approving inflated invoices for non-existent goods and services. The fraud was uncovered when inconsistencies in supply chain records triggered an internal audit. The company suffered financial losses, supplier disputes, and regulatory investigations. To prevent recurrence, SOD policies were reinforced by ensuring that supplier selection, contract approvals, and financial disbursements were handled by separate teams. Automated procurement platforms were introduced with built-in approval workflows and transaction monitoring to detect anomalies in vendor payments.

An energy company faced an operational shutdown due to unauthorized modifications made to critical control systems. Engineers responsible for infrastructure maintenance had excessive privileges, allowing them to bypass safety protocols and execute changes without independent review. One engineer made an undocumented modification to a power grid control system, leading to a cascading failure that resulted in widespread power outages. Investigations revealed that SOD policies were not enforced, and real-time monitoring of privileged activities was lacking. The incident led to regulatory scrutiny and mandatory safety reforms. To strengthen security, the company implemented Privileged Access Management (PAM) solutions, requiring multi-person approval for all system modifications. AI-driven behavior analytics were deployed to detect unusual activity in real time, preventing unauthorized infrastructure changes.

A multinational investment firm faced a high-profile scandal after a trader exploited weak SOD controls to conduct unauthorized transactions that resulted in significant financial losses. The trader had access to both the trading system and the risk management tools, allowing unauthorized trades to bypass detection. The firm did not have a secondary review process for high-risk transactions, and manual audits failed to identify the issue until the losses had already accumulated. Following the incident, the investment firm restructured its trading workflows, ensuring that all high-value transactions required independent verification from a separate risk management team. Automated monitoring systems were implemented to flag unusual trading behavior and enforce real-time transaction approvals.

These case studies illustrate the consequences of failing to enforce SOD in various industries, highlighting the risks of excessive access privileges, inadequate oversight, and lack of real-time monitoring. Organizations must learn from these failures by implementing automated access controls, enforcing role-based restrictions, conducting regular access reviews, and integrating real-time anomaly detection systems. Strengthening SOD policies ensures better security, regulatory compliance, and operational integrity, reducing the risk of financial fraud, data breaches, and insider threats.

SOD and Insider Threat Management

Segregation of Duties (SOD) plays a crucial role in managing insider threats by ensuring that no single individual has excessive control over critical business processes, financial transactions, or sensitive data. Insider threats can originate from employees, contractors, or business partners who exploit their access privileges for malicious activities, financial gain, espionage, or sabotage. Without proper SOD enforcement, organizations are vulnerable to fraud, unauthorized access, data breaches, and operational disruptions caused by insiders who have unchecked authority over multiple functions. Implementing strong SOD policies helps limit the potential damage insiders can inflict by ensuring that key tasks require multiple individuals for approval, reducing the risk of privilege abuse.

One of the primary ways SOD mitigates insider threats is by separating high-risk responsibilities within an organization. In financial systems, an employee should not have the ability to initiate and approve payments, as this could enable fraudulent transactions without oversight. Similarly, in IT environments, a system administrator should not have the ability to create user accounts, modify security logs, and approve their own changes. By requiring different individuals to handle separate functions, SOD ensures that no single insider can carry out unauthorized activities without detection. This separation of duties not only prevents intentional fraud but also reduces the risk of accidental errors caused by employees with excessive access privileges.

Organizations that fail to enforce SOD effectively often experience insider-driven fraud and security breaches. Many high-profile cases of financial fraud, such as embezzlement schemes and unauthorized fund transfers, have occurred due to weak access controls that allowed insiders to bypass oversight mechanisms. By implementing SOD policies that require dual approvals for financial transactions and restricting access to critical accounts, organizations can significantly reduce the likelihood of insider fraud. Automated access control systems further enhance security by enforcing role-based permissions, ensuring that employees cannot accumulate conflicting privileges over time.

Privileged access management (PAM) is a key component of SOD enforcement in mitigating insider threats. Employees with elevated privileges, such as IT administrators, database managers, and finance officers, pose a higher risk due to their ability to bypass security controls. PAM solutions enforce least privilege access by granting temporary, just-in-time (JIT) privileges rather than providing permanent administrative access. By requiring multi-factor authentication (MFA) and logging all privileged activities, PAM solutions create accountability and reduce the risk of insider abuse. Continuous monitoring of privileged users helps detect unusual behavior, such as unauthorized modifications to critical systems or repeated access attempts outside normal work hours.

Real-time monitoring and anomaly detection are essential for identifying insider threats before they escalate into major security incidents. Machine learning and AI-driven analytics can analyze user behavior, detect deviations from normal access patterns, and flag suspicious activities. For example, if an employee who normally accesses customer records suddenly begins downloading large amounts of sensitive data, an automated alert can be triggered for security review. Security Information and Event Management (SIEM) systems integrate with IAM and SOD policies to provide centralized visibility into user activities, ensuring that unauthorized actions are promptly detected and investigated.

SOD enforcement also plays a vital role in protecting intellectual property and sensitive business information from insider threats. In industries such as pharmaceuticals, technology, and defense, employees often have access to proprietary research, trade secrets, and confidential project data. Without proper SOD controls, insiders could copy, alter, or leak sensitive information without detection. By enforcing strict access controls, requiring multi-person approvals for data transfers, and restricting access to critical files based on job roles, organizations can prevent unauthorized disclosures. Data loss prevention (DLP) solutions further enhance security by monitoring and blocking unauthorized attempts to share or exfiltrate sensitive files.

Supply chain security is another area where SOD helps mitigate insider threats. Employees involved in procurement, vendor management, and logistics operations have access to supply chain data, financial records, and contract approvals. If a single individual is responsible for supplier selection, purchase order approvals, and invoice payments, there is a high risk of fraud, kickbacks, or conflicts of interest. By enforcing SOD policies that separate supplier evaluation, financial approvals, and payment processing, organizations can reduce the risk of fraudulent transactions. Blockchain technology is increasingly being used to enhance supply chain transparency, ensuring that all transactions are independently verified and immutable.

Insider threats also extend to physical security, where unauthorized access to restricted areas, equipment, or sensitive documents can lead to security breaches. SOD policies ensure that no single employee has unrestricted access to secure facilities, preventing unauthorized tampering or theft. Badge access controls, biometric authentication, and security checkpoints reinforce SOD by ensuring that sensitive areas require dual authentication or supervisor approval. Security audits and access reviews further help organizations detect and prevent unauthorized access to restricted locations.

Training and awareness programs are essential for ensuring that employees understand the importance of SOD and their role in preventing insider threats. Many insider security incidents occur due to negligence rather than malicious intent, with employees unintentionally violating access policies or failing to recognize security risks. Regular training sessions on SOD principles, access control best practices, and recognizing suspicious behavior help create a security-conscious workforce. Encouraging employees to report potential insider threats through anonymous reporting mechanisms also strengthens SOD enforcement by enabling early detection of suspicious activities.

Regulatory compliance is a major driver of SOD enforcement in insider threat management. Organizations subject to regulations such as the Sarbanes-Oxley Act (SOX), the General Data Protection Regulation (GDPR), and the Health Insurance Portability and Accountability Act (HIPAA) must implement strict access controls to prevent insider-driven fraud and data breaches. Regulatory audits often focus on whether organizations have implemented effective SOD policies, maintained access logs, and conducted regular reviews of user privileges. Compliance automation tools help organizations track access control violations, generate audit reports, and ensure adherence to industry regulations.

Organizations must also continuously refine their SOD policies and insider threat detection strategies to adapt to evolving risks. As businesses adopt cloud-based applications, remote work models, and digital transformation initiatives, SOD enforcement must extend beyond traditional on-premises environments. Cloud Identity and Access Management (Cloud IAM) solutions provide centralized control over user access across multiple platforms, ensuring that SOD policies are consistently applied. Continuous monitoring, AI-driven risk assessments, and real-time threat intelligence further enhance SOD enforcement by identifying emerging insider threats and enabling proactive security responses.

By integrating SOD with insider threat management strategies, organizations can create a robust security framework that protects financial assets, sensitive data, and critical business operations from internal risks. Implementing role-based access controls, privileged access management, real-time monitoring, data loss prevention, supply chain security measures, and security training programs ensures that organizations can effectively detect, prevent, and mitigate insider threats. Strengthening SOD policies not only reduces security risks but also reinforces compliance, operational integrity, and trust within the organization.

Third-Party Access and SOD Considerations

Third-party access introduces significant security and compliance challenges for organizations, particularly in environments where Segregation of Duties (SOD) policies are critical for preventing fraud, data breaches, and regulatory violations. Vendors, contractors, consultants, suppliers, and service providers often require access to internal systems, sensitive data, and business processes to fulfill their roles. However, without strict SOD controls, these external users can accumulate excessive privileges, create conflicts of interest, and bypass critical security controls. Managing third-party access while ensuring SOD compliance requires a combination of robust access management strategies, continuous monitoring, and well-defined policies to minimize security risks and maintain operational integrity.

One of the primary challenges of third-party access is the lack of direct oversight and accountability. Unlike internal employees, external users operate outside the organization's direct control, making it difficult to enforce access restrictions and monitor their activities effectively. Many organizations provide vendors and contractors with privileged access to IT systems, cloud applications, and databases without properly restricting their permissions. This unrestricted access increases the risk of insider threats, unauthorized data modifications, and policy violations. To mitigate these risks, organizations must enforce least privilege access by granting third-party users only the permissions necessary to perform their tasks while ensuring that no single external user has conflicting privileges.

Role-based access control (RBAC) is a fundamental mechanism for enforcing SOD policies in third-party access management. Organizations must define clear roles for vendors, contractors, and external service providers based on their specific job functions and responsibilities. Each role should have predefined permissions aligned with SOD principles, ensuring that external users cannot perform conflicting actions. For example, a third-party IT support provider responsible for software updates should not have access to financial transaction systems, preventing unauthorized financial modifications. By implementing strict role assignments, organizations can prevent third-party users from accumulating excessive privileges over time, reducing the risk of policy violations.

Privileged access management (PAM) is essential for securing third-party access, particularly when vendors and contractors require administrative privileges to perform maintenance, troubleshooting, or system configurations. Many organizations fail to enforce adequate PAM controls, allowing external IT personnel unrestricted access to critical infrastructure, cloud environments, and security settings. Without proper oversight, third-party administrators can introduce security vulnerabilities, modify configurations without approval, or escalate their own privileges to bypass security controls. Implementing just-in-time (JIT) privileged access ensures that third-party users receive temporary, time-limited administrative permissions only when necessary. Additionally, session monitoring and audit logging help track all privileged activities, providing real-time visibility into third-party actions.

Cloud-based third-party access presents additional challenges in SOD enforcement due to the decentralized nature of cloud environments. Organizations relying on multiple cloud service providers (CSPs) must ensure that external users do not have conflicting permissions across different platforms. Cloud Identity and Access Management (Cloud IAM) solutions help enforce SOD policies by centralizing access control, defining least privilege access, and preventing unauthorized privilege escalation. Organizations should regularly review and revoke unnecessary cloud access for third-party users to reduce security risks. Multi-factor authentication (MFA) should also be enforced for all external users accessing cloud systems to prevent unauthorized logins.

Supply chain security is another critical area where SOD policies must be enforced for third-party access. Organizations rely on external suppliers, logistics providers, and manufacturing partners who require access to procurement systems, inventory databases, and financial transactions. If SOD controls are not properly implemented, third-party vendors could manipulate procurement records, alter pricing structures, or engage in fraudulent transactions. Organizations must ensure that supplier evaluation, contract approval, and payment processing functions are handled by separate teams, reducing the risk of conflicts of interest. Automated procurement systems integrated with SOD enforcement mechanisms help detect unauthorized modifications and flag suspicious vendor activities.

Regulatory compliance is a key factor driving the need for strict SOD enforcement in third-party access management. Many industries are subject to regulations such as the General Data Protection Regulation (GDPR), the Sarbanes-Oxley Act (SOX), the Health Insurance Portability and Accountability Act (HIPAA), and the Payment Card Industry Data Security Standard (PCI DSS), all of which require organizations to maintain strict access controls and prevent unauthorized transactions. Regulatory auditors often scrutinize third-party access management policies to ensure compliance with data protection and financial security standards. Organizations must maintain detailed audit logs of third-party activities, regularly review access permissions, and enforce SOD policies to meet compliance requirements.

Continuous monitoring and real-time threat detection are critical for preventing third-party users from violating SOD policies. Many security breaches occur when external vendors or contractors gain excessive access, either intentionally or due to misconfigurations. Organizations must deploy Security Information and Event Management (SIEM) solutions to monitor third-party activities, detect unauthorized access attempts, and generate alerts for suspicious behavior. AI-driven anomaly detection tools further enhance monitoring by identifying deviations from normal access patterns. For example, if a third-party vendor attempts to access financial systems outside of their assigned role, an automated alert can notify security teams to investigate the incident.

Third-party access reviews should be conducted regularly to ensure that external users do not retain privileges longer than necessary. Many organizations fail to revoke vendor access after project completion, leading to unnecessary security risks. IAM solutions with automated access certification workflows help streamline third-party access reviews by generating reports on active external accounts, highlighting excessive privileges, and enforcing access expiration dates. By conducting periodic reviews, organizations can ensure that third-party users only have access to systems for the duration required, reducing the risk of privilege misuse.

Vendor risk assessments should be integrated into third-party access management strategies to evaluate the security practices of external partners. Organizations must assess whether third-party vendors comply with SOD requirements, enforce strong access controls, and follow cybersecurity best practices. Contracts with vendors should include security clauses that require adherence to SOD policies, regular access audits, and prompt reporting of security incidents. Third-party risk management platforms help organizations assess vendor security postures, track compliance metrics, and enforce contractual security obligations.

Security training and awareness programs should be extended to third-party users to ensure that they understand SOD policies, access control requirements, and security best practices. Many security incidents result from negligence or human error rather than malicious intent. Vendors and contractors should receive training on secure access procedures, phishing awareness, and compliance requirements before being granted system access. Organizations should also implement strict onboarding and offboarding processes to ensure that third-party access is granted only after security training is completed and revoked immediately upon contract termination.

By enforcing strong SOD policies, implementing role-based access control, leveraging privileged access management, continuously monitoring third-party activities, and integrating vendor risk management strategies, organizations can mitigate security risks associated with third-party access. A well-defined third-party access governance framework ensures that external users do not accumulate conflicting privileges, prevents unauthorized modifications to critical systems, and maintains compliance with regulatory requirements. As organizations continue to expand their reliance on third-party vendors, ensuring proper SOD enforcement remains a critical component of securing business operations, protecting sensitive data, and maintaining trust in external partnerships.

Vendor Risk Management and SOD

Vendor risk management and segregation of duties (SOD) are closely connected in ensuring that third-party service providers, contractors, and suppliers do not introduce security, financial, or compliance risks to an organization. As businesses increasingly rely on external vendors for critical services, the need to enforce strict access controls, mitigate conflicts of interest, and prevent unauthorized activities becomes essential. Without proper SOD policies in place, vendors can accumulate excessive privileges, bypass security measures, and create vulnerabilities that could be exploited by malicious actors. A comprehensive vendor risk management framework integrated with SOD controls helps organizations maintain security, regulatory compliance, and operational integrity while working with third-party partners.

One of the biggest challenges in vendor risk management is the lack of direct oversight over external entities. Unlike internal employees, vendors operate outside the organization's direct control, making it more difficult to monitor their actions, enforce policies, and ensure accountability. Many security breaches and financial fraud incidents have occurred due to vendors gaining excessive privileges, failing to follow security best practices, or intentionally bypassing controls. Implementing strict SOD policies for vendor access ensures that no single third-party user has unchecked authority over critical business functions. Organizations must carefully define roles and responsibilities, ensuring that vendors cannot initiate, approve, and execute transactions without independent verification.

Access control is a critical component of vendor risk management and SOD enforcement. Organizations must ensure that vendors only receive the minimum level of access required to perform their specific job functions. Role-based access control (RBAC) frameworks help enforce these restrictions by assigning predefined roles with limited permissions to vendors based on their contractual obligations. For example, a third-party IT support provider should only have access to technical troubleshooting tools but should not be able to modify security configurations or financial records. Access requests should undergo strict approval processes, requiring multiple levels of authorization before privileges are granted to external users.

Privileged access management (PAM) plays a crucial role in enforcing SOD for vendor access. Many vendors require administrative access to IT infrastructure, cloud environments, or critical business applications to perform maintenance, software updates, or security assessments.

Without proper PAM controls, vendors can exploit their elevated privileges to manipulate systems, introduce security vulnerabilities, or exfiltrate sensitive data. Organizations must enforce just-in-time (JIT) access provisioning, ensuring that vendors receive temporary, role-based privileges that expire once their tasks are completed. Multi-factor authentication (MFA), session monitoring, and detailed activity logs further enhance security by tracking vendor interactions and preventing unauthorized modifications.

Regulatory compliance is a major driver of SOD enforcement in vendor risk management. Organizations in highly regulated industries, such as finance, healthcare, and manufacturing, must ensure that vendor activities align with legal requirements, including the General Data Protection Regulation (GDPR), Sarbanes-Oxley Act (SOX), Payment Card Industry Data Security Standard (PCI DSS), and Health Insurance Portability and Accountability Act (HIPAA). Regulatory audits often scrutinize third-party access controls, requiring organizations to demonstrate that vendors do not have conflicting privileges that could lead to fraudulent transactions or data breaches. Automated compliance tracking tools help organizations document vendor access, generate audit reports, and ensure that SOD policies are consistently enforced across all vendor relationships.

Third-party risk assessments are essential for identifying potential security threats and compliance gaps before vendors gain access to critical systems. Organizations must conduct thorough due diligence when onboarding new vendors, evaluating their security posture, access control policies, and history of regulatory compliance. Vendor risk management platforms automate this process by assessing vendor security practices, monitoring threat intelligence sources, and assigning risk scores to third-party providers. High-risk vendors should undergo additional scrutiny, requiring more restrictive access controls, enhanced monitoring, and frequent security assessments. Continuous risk assessments ensure that vendors maintain compliance with evolving security standards and regulatory requirements throughout their engagement.

Vendor contract management must incorporate SOD principles to enforce accountability and mitigate risks associated with external service providers. Contracts should include specific security clauses that outline access restrictions, data protection requirements, and compliance obligations. Service Level Agreements (SLAs) should define clear responsibilities for vendors, ensuring that access privileges are granted based on the principle of least privilege. Organizations should also include termination clauses that require immediate access revocation and secure data deletion upon contract expiration. Regular contract reviews help organizations adapt to changes in vendor risk profiles, ensuring that SOD controls remain aligned with business needs and security requirements.

Continuous monitoring and real-time threat detection are critical for preventing vendor-related security incidents. Many data breaches occur when vendors are granted excessive access, either intentionally or due to misconfigurations. Organizations must deploy Security Information and Event Management (SIEM) solutions to monitor vendor activities, detect policy violations, and trigger alerts for suspicious behavior. AI-driven analytics enhance monitoring by identifying anomalous access patterns, such as vendors attempting to access unauthorized systems or downloading excessive amounts of data. Automated response mechanisms, such as access revocation or additional authentication challenges, help mitigate risks in real-time.

Periodic vendor access reviews help organizations maintain SOD enforcement and ensure that vendors do not retain privileges beyond their required time frame. Many organizations fail to conduct regular reviews, leading to vendor accounts remaining active long after contractual engagements end. IAM solutions with automated access certification workflows streamline the review process by generating reports on active vendor accounts, flagging excessive privileges, and enforcing expiration dates for temporary access. Vendor access should be reassessed at predefined intervals to ensure that external users only have access to necessary systems, reducing the risk of unauthorized privilege accumulation.

Supply chain security is another area where SOD policies must be integrated into vendor risk management. Organizations rely on external suppliers, logistics providers, and manufacturing partners who require access to procurement systems, inventory databases, and financial transactions. If SOD controls are not properly implemented, vendors could engage in fraudulent activities, such as altering

148

procurement records, manipulating pricing structures, or bypassing contract approval workflows. Organizations must separate vendor evaluation, contract approval, and payment processing functions to prevent conflicts of interest. Automated procurement systems with SOD enforcement mechanisms help detect unauthorized modifications, reducing the risk of supply chain fraud.

Vendor security training and awareness programs further support SOD enforcement by educating external users on access control best practices, cybersecurity risks, and compliance requirements. Many security incidents arise from vendor negligence rather than malicious intent. Providing mandatory security training for vendors before granting access to critical systems ensures that they understand their responsibilities and the consequences of policy violations. Regular security awareness programs help reinforce compliance expectations and reduce the likelihood of vendor-related security breaches.

A well-structured vendor risk management program that integrates SOD policies enhances security, reduces third-party risks, and ensures compliance with industry regulations. By implementing strict access controls, enforcing role-based restrictions, leveraging privileged access management, continuously monitoring vendor activities, and conducting regular risk assessments, organizations can prevent vendors from accumulating excessive privileges or engaging in unauthorized activities. As businesses continue to expand their reliance on third-party partnerships, maintaining strong SOD enforcement remains a critical component of protecting sensitive data, securing IT environments, and safeguarding business operations.

SOD in Mergers and Acquisitions

Segregation of Duties (SOD) is a crucial factor in maintaining security, compliance, and operational integrity during mergers and acquisitions (M&A). When two organizations combine, they must integrate their financial systems, IT environments, access controls, and governance policies while ensuring that no individual or department gains excessive control over critical business functions. Without proper SOD enforcement, M&A activities can introduce security risks, financial fraud, insider threats, and regulatory violations. Effective SOD policies help mitigate these risks by ensuring that key responsibilities are distributed among multiple individuals, preventing unauthorized access, and maintaining transparency throughout the integration process.

One of the primary challenges in M&A transactions is the consolidation of financial systems and approval workflows. Each organization has its own financial controls, vendor contracts, and payment authorization mechanisms that must be harmonized. Without enforcing proper SOD, employees from either organization may accumulate conflicting roles, allowing them to manipulate financial transactions without oversight. For example, an individual with access to both accounts payable and financial reconciliation processes could exploit this overlap to approve fraudulent payments. To mitigate these risks, organizations must conduct a thorough SOD review of financial functions, ensuring that payment approvals, budget allocations, and financial audits are handled by separate personnel.

Access control integration is another critical aspect of SOD enforcement in M&A. Organizations merging their IT environments must reconcile different identity and access management (IAM) systems, ensuring that users from both entities do not inherit conflicting privileges. Inconsistent access controls can lead to unauthorized data exposure, security breaches, or privilege escalation risks. A structured approach to IAM integration includes role-based access control (RBAC) reviews, privileged access assessments, and automated access reconciliation processes. Temporary access restrictions may be necessary during the transition phase to prevent unauthorized cross-system modifications until new governance policies are fully implemented.

Privileged Access Management (PAM) is essential in M&A activities to prevent insider threats and unauthorized administrative actions. IT administrators, finance executives, and compliance officers from both organizations require elevated access to manage the integration of enterprise systems. If privileged users have unrestricted control over both organizations' infrastructure, they could bypass security controls, alter financial records, or manipulate data migrations. Implementing just-in-time (JIT) privileged access, requiring multi-factor authentication (MFA), and enforcing real-time monitoring ensures that all administrative actions are properly authorized and logged. Security Information and Event Management (SIEM) solutions help detect anomalies in privileged access activity, preventing unauthorized system modifications.

Regulatory compliance is a major concern in M&A, requiring strict enforcement of SOD policies to align with industry regulations such as the Sarbanes-Oxley Act (SOX), General Data Protection Regulation (GDPR), and Payment Card Industry Data Security Standard (PCI DSS). Regulatory bodies closely monitor M&A transactions, requiring organizations to demonstrate strong internal controls over financial reporting, data privacy, and cybersecurity. SOD compliance ensures that financial statements remain accurate and that no single employee has control over both data entry and verification processes. Automated compliance tracking tools streamline audit preparations by generating reports on access controls, transaction approvals, and security policy enforcement.

Data migration and system consolidation present additional SOD challenges during M&A. Organizations must transfer vast amounts of sensitive data, including financial records, customer information, and intellectual property, while ensuring that no individual has unilateral control over data transfers and modifications. Without SOD enforcement, malicious insiders could alter data integrity, delete audit logs, or exfiltrate confidential information. Implementing strict approval workflows for data migrations, enforcing access restrictions, and monitoring file transfers in real-time mitigates the risk of unauthorized data manipulation. Encryption and digital signing mechanisms further enhance data integrity, ensuring that only authorized users can access or modify critical records.

Vendor and third-party risk management require careful SOD considerations in M&A transactions. Both organizations have established vendor relationships, third-party contracts, and supply chain dependencies that must be reviewed and integrated. If vendor approvals, procurement functions, and financial disbursements are not properly segregated, there is an increased risk of fraudulent transactions, duplicate payments, or contractual conflicts. Organizations must conduct thorough vendor access reviews, ensuring that third-party users do not retain unnecessary privileges across the merged entity. Automated vendor risk assessment platforms help track third-party access, flag high-risk vendors, and enforce compliance with updated SOD policies.

Human resource management during M&A also necessitates strong SOD enforcement to prevent payroll fraud, unauthorized role assignments, and conflicts of interest. Employees from both organizations require re-evaluation of their roles, ensuring that no individual retains excessive access to HR, payroll, or employee benefits systems. If a single user has the ability to modify salaries, approve payments, and alter employee records, there is a heightened risk of financial fraud. IAM solutions integrated with HR systems provide automated role reassignment capabilities, ensuring that access privileges are aligned with updated job functions and organizational structures.

Continuous monitoring and audit logging are essential for detecting potential SOD violations during the M&A process. As access control policies and governance structures evolve, organizations must proactively monitor user activity across integrated systems. SIEM and AI-driven security analytics help identify unusual transaction patterns, unauthorized access attempts, and privilege escalations. By implementing real-time alerts and automated response mechanisms, organizations can quickly mitigate insider threats and prevent fraudulent activities. Regular security audits ensure that SOD policies remain effective throughout the transition period and beyond.

Training and awareness programs support SOD enforcement by educating employees on access control policies, compliance requirements, and security best practices. During M&A, employees may inadvertently violate SOD policies due to a lack of understanding of new governance frameworks. Organizations should conduct mandatory training sessions for employees, IT administrators, and finance teams to reinforce the importance of SOD compliance. Security awareness campaigns help prevent accidental data exposure, unauthorized system modifications, and access control misconfigurations. By fostering a culture of accountability, organizations can ensure that employees actively participate in maintaining SOD integrity during the transition.

As M&A activities continue to grow in complexity, organizations must prioritize SOD enforcement to mitigate financial risks, prevent security breaches, and ensure regulatory compliance. By implementing strict access controls, segregating financial functions, securing privileged access, continuously monitoring system activity, and educating employees, organizations can successfully integrate their operations while minimizing SOD-related vulnerabilities. A well-structured SOD framework provides the necessary checks and balances to maintain transparency, prevent fraud, and establish a secure foundation for the newly merged entity.

SOD and Zero Trust Security Frameworks

Segregation of Duties (SOD) and Zero Trust security frameworks are two essential components of a robust cybersecurity strategy. Both aim to minimize security risks by restricting unauthorized access, enforcing strict controls, and ensuring accountability in business processes. SOD is traditionally used to prevent fraud, insider threats, and conflicts of interest by ensuring that no single individual has control over critical transactions or functions. Zero Trust, on the other hand, assumes that no user, system, or device should be inherently trusted, requiring continuous authentication, least privilege access, and real-time monitoring. Integrating SOD with a Zero Trust security model strengthens an organization's security posture by reinforcing access control mechanisms, preventing privilege misuse, and ensuring that users only have access to the resources necessary for their roles.

One of the fundamental principles of Zero Trust is least privilege access, which aligns with SOD by restricting user permissions to the minimum level required to perform their job functions. Traditional access control models often grant users broad permissions, leading to privilege accumulation and increasing the risk of unauthorized actions. Zero Trust enforces least privilege dynamically by continuously evaluating user behavior, access context, and risk levels. In an SOD framework, this means that employees, contractors, and third-party vendors cannot perform conflicting duties or escalate their privileges without proper authorization. Organizations implementing Zero Trust principles must ensure that SOD policies are embedded into access control models to prevent unauthorized privilege escalation.

Identity and Access Management (IAM) plays a critical role in integrating SOD with Zero Trust security. In a Zero Trust model, authentication and authorization are continuously verified, requiring strong identity controls to ensure that users do not exceed their authorized permissions. Role-based access control (RBAC) and attribute-based access control (ABAC) are commonly used in SOD enforcement to prevent users from gaining conflicting roles. Zero Trust enhances these controls by enforcing risk-based authentication, requiring additional verification steps when users attempt to access sensitive resources. For example, if an employee with financial approval rights tries to modify vendor payment details, Zero Trust policies may trigger multi-factor authentication (MFA) or require additional approvals before granting access.

Privileged Access Management (PAM) is another essential component of Zero Trust security that strengthens SOD enforcement. Privileged accounts, such as IT administrators, finance executives, and security analysts, pose a higher risk due to their elevated permissions. Without proper governance, privileged users can bypass SOD controls, modify security settings, or access sensitive data without oversight. Zero Trust enforces strict privileged access controls by requiring just-in-time (JIT) privilege elevation, real-time session monitoring, and continuous access validation. By integrating PAM with SOD policies, organizations ensure that privileged users do not perform conflicting duties, such as approving their own financial transactions or modifying audit logs.

Continuous monitoring and real-time threat detection are critical for enforcing SOD in a Zero Trust framework. Traditional SOD reviews rely on periodic audits and static access control rules, which may not detect real-time security violations. Zero Trust security enhances SOD by continuously analyzing user behavior, identifying anomalies, and triggering automated responses to potential violations. Security Information and Event Management (SIEM) solutions, combined with AI-driven analytics, help detect unauthorized access attempts, privilege escalations, and suspicious transactions. If an employee attempts to override financial approval workflows or modify security policies outside their designated role, Zero Trust controls can immediately revoke access, generate alerts, and initiate an investigation.

Network segmentation is another key aspect of Zero Trust that supports SOD enforcement by limiting lateral movement within an organization's infrastructure. Traditional network security models often assume that users inside the corporate network are trustworthy, granting them broad access to internal systems. Zero Trust eliminates this assumption by enforcing micro-segmentation, restricting users to specific resources based on their roles and access needs. In an SOD framework, this prevents users from gaining unauthorized access to systems outside their designated responsibilities. For example, an HR employee with payroll access should not have visibility into financial reporting systems, and a developer working on application code should not have access to production environments. Micro-segmentation ensures that users can only interact with the resources necessary for their specific job functions.

Cloud security and Zero Trust models further enhance SOD enforcement in hybrid and multi-cloud environments. As organizations adopt cloud-based applications, traditional perimeter-based security models become ineffective in preventing unauthorized access. Zero Trust ensures that cloud users are continuously authenticated and authorized, preventing unauthorized privilege escalation. Cloud IAM solutions enforce SOD policies by dynamically assigning access permissions based on user behavior, risk scores, and contextual attributes such as device security posture and geolocation. If a third-party contractor working remotely requests access to financial approval systems, Zero Trust policies may enforce additional authentication requirements, such as device verification or time-restricted access windows.

Data protection and encryption are integral to SOD and Zero Trust security frameworks, ensuring that sensitive information remains secure even if unauthorized access occurs. Zero Trust enforces strict data access policies, requiring users to verify their identities before accessing confidential files. In an SOD model, this prevents unauthorized data modifications, fraudulent financial transactions, and regulatory compliance violations. Data Loss Prevention (DLP) solutions integrated with Zero Trust policies monitor data access attempts, detect unusual file modifications, and prevent unauthorized data transfers. For example, if an employee with payroll processing privileges attempts to export sensitive employee salary data, Zero Trust controls can block the transaction and generate a security alert.

Regulatory compliance is another key driver of SOD and Zero Trust integration, as organizations must adhere to strict industry standards such as the General Data Protection Regulation (GDPR), Sarbanes-Oxley Act (SOX), and Payment Card Industry Data Security Standard (PCI DSS). These regulations require organizations to enforce access controls, maintain audit logs, and prevent unauthorized privilege escalation. Zero Trust enhances compliance by providing continuous access verification, automated compliance reporting, and real-time audit trails. Organizations implementing Zero Trust security can demonstrate stronger SOD enforcement during regulatory audits, reducing the risk of compliance violations and financial penalties.

Employee training and security awareness programs support the integration of SOD and Zero Trust by ensuring that users understand access control policies, security best practices, and compliance requirements. Many security breaches occur due to human error, such as employees sharing credentials, bypassing security controls, or failing to recognize phishing attacks. Zero Trust security enforces strict authentication policies, but employees must be educated on the importance of adhering to access control principles. Security awareness programs should include training on role-based access management, privileged account security, and recognizing suspicious activities that may indicate insider threats or unauthorized access attempts.

As cybersecurity threats continue to evolve, integrating SOD with Zero Trust security frameworks provides organizations with a powerful defense against insider threats, unauthorized access, and regulatory non-compliance. By enforcing least privilege access, continuously monitoring user activities, leveraging AI-driven threat detection, and securing cloud environments, organizations can ensure that users only have access to the resources necessary for their roles. A Zero Trust security model strengthens SOD policies by eliminating implicit trust, enforcing strict authentication requirements, and dynamically adapting security controls based on real-time risk assessments.

Through the combination of SOD and Zero Trust, organizations can achieve greater security, operational integrity, and compliance resilience in an increasingly complex threat landscape.

Identity Lifecycle Management and SOD

Identity lifecycle management (ILM) plays a crucial role in enforcing segregation of duties (SOD) by ensuring that user identities are properly created, maintained, and deactivated throughout their lifecycle within an organization. ILM governs how identities are provisioned, modified, and deprovisioned, ensuring that users have the appropriate level of access at each stage of their employment or contractual engagement. Without proper identity lifecycle management, organizations risk accumulating excessive privileges, conflicting access rights, and unauthorized system access, all of which can lead to fraud, security breaches, and regulatory non-compliance. Integrating SOD policies into identity lifecycle management frameworks helps prevent unauthorized privilege accumulation, ensures accountability, and maintains compliance with internal policies and industry regulations.

Provisioning is the first stage of identity lifecycle management and is critical for enforcing SOD from the moment a user joins an organization. During the onboarding process, new employees, contractors, and third-party users must be assigned appropriate roles and access privileges based on their job responsibilities. If provisioning is not controlled with SOD in mind, users may be granted excessive or conflicting access, leading to security risks. Role-based access control (RBAC) and attribute-based access control (ABAC) frameworks help enforce SOD by ensuring that users receive only the necessary permissions for their roles. Automated provisioning workflows integrated with SOD policies prevent users from acquiring conflicting roles, such as the ability to both initiate and approve financial transactions.

Access requests and modifications during the identity lifecycle must be carefully managed to prevent SOD violations. Employees often require changes to their access permissions due to job transfers, promotions, or project-based assignments. Without proper oversight, access modifications can lead to privilege accumulation, where users retain access to previous roles while gaining new permissions. This creates the risk of users being able to bypass approval processes, manipulate data, or engage in fraudulent activities. Automated access request management systems enforce SOD by requiring approvals from multiple stakeholders before access modifications are granted. Risk-based access reviews ensure that any changes in permissions are evaluated against SOD policies to prevent conflicts of interest.

Privileged access management (PAM) is a critical aspect of identity lifecycle management that ensures users with elevated privileges do not violate SOD policies. Privileged users, such as IT administrators, security analysts, and finance executives, often require high-level access to perform their duties. However, without strict governance, these users can exploit their privileges to bypass controls, modify security settings, or alter financial records. Implementing just-in-time (JIT) privileged access, requiring multi-factor authentication (MFA), and continuously monitoring privileged sessions help enforce SOD. PAM solutions ensure that privileged users cannot perform conflicting actions, such as approving their own administrative changes or modifying audit logs without oversight.

Periodic access reviews are essential in identity lifecycle management to ensure that users maintain only the necessary permissions and do not accumulate conflicting privileges over time. Many organizations fail to conduct regular reviews, leading to employees retaining access to systems they no longer need. This increases the risk of SOD violations and insider threats. Automated access certification processes enforce SOD by periodically validating user access rights and requiring managers to review and approve ongoing access. If conflicting privileges are detected, corrective actions such as access revocation or role reassignment must be taken to maintain compliance with SOD policies.

Deprovisioning is a critical phase of identity lifecycle management that ensures former employees, contractors, and third-party users do not retain access to organizational systems after their departure. Failure to properly deprovision identities can lead to unauthorized access, security breaches, and compliance violations. Inadequate deprovisioning processes have led to real-world security incidents where former employees exploited lingering access rights to steal sensitive data or manipulate financial transactions. Automated deprovisioning workflows enforce SOD by ensuring that access is revoked immediately upon user departure, reducing the risk of unauthorized activities. Integration with HR systems ensures that terminations trigger automatic access removal across all applications and IT environments.

Identity federation and single sign-on (SSO) solutions further enhance SOD enforcement by centralizing identity management across multiple systems and platforms. Organizations often use a combination of on-premises applications, cloud-based services, and third-party platforms, each with its own access controls. Without centralized identity management, users may acquire conflicting privileges across different environments, leading to SOD violations. Identity federation ensures that user authentication and authorization policies remain consistent across all systems, preventing unauthorized privilege escalation. SSO solutions enforce SOD by allowing users to authenticate once while maintaining strict access control policies that prevent conflicting access assignments.

Real-time monitoring and anomaly detection strengthen SOD enforcement within identity lifecycle management by identifying suspicious user activity. Traditional access control models rely on static rules and periodic audits, which may not detect real-time violations. AI-driven behavior analytics and machine learning models enhance security by continuously analyzing user actions and flagging anomalies that indicate potential SOD breaches. If a user suddenly attempts to access financial approval systems after being assigned a conflicting role, real-time alerts can notify security teams for immediate investigation. Security Information and Event Management (SIEM) systems further support SOD enforcement by aggregating access logs, correlating security events, and providing forensic analysis of unauthorized activities.

Regulatory compliance requirements drive the need for integrating SOD with identity lifecycle management. Organizations in highly regulated industries, such as finance, healthcare, and government, must comply with laws such as the Sarbanes-Oxley Act (SOX), the

General Data Protection Regulation (GDPR), and the Health Insurance Portability and Accountability Act (HIPAA). These regulations mandate strict access controls, audit trails, and periodic access reviews to prevent fraud, unauthorized transactions, and data breaches. Automated compliance tracking tools help organizations enforce SOD by ensuring that identity management processes align with regulatory mandates. Audit-ready reports provide visibility into user access rights, policy violations, and corrective actions taken to maintain compliance.

Employee training and security awareness programs further support SOD enforcement within identity lifecycle management by educating users on the importance of access control, privilege separation, and security best practices. Many access control violations occur due to human error, negligence, or lack of awareness rather than malicious intent. Organizations should conduct regular training sessions to ensure that employees, IT administrators, and managers understand SOD principles, identity lifecycle policies, and compliance requirements. Security awareness programs reinforce the importance of proper access request procedures, password hygiene, and recognizing potential insider threats.

A well-structured identity lifecycle management framework that integrates SOD policies enhances security, prevents fraud, and ensures regulatory compliance. By enforcing least privilege access, continuously monitoring user activities, automating access reviews, securing privileged accounts, and educating employees, organizations can maintain strict control over identity and access governance. A proactive approach to SOD within identity lifecycle management reduces security risks, strengthens compliance efforts, and ensures operational integrity across all business functions.

Self-Service IAM and Its Impact on SOD

Self-service Identity and Access Management (IAM) solutions have become an essential component of modern IT environments, enabling employees, contractors, and third-party users to manage their own access requests, password resets, and role assignments without requiring direct intervention from IT administrators. While self-service IAM improves operational efficiency, enhances user experience, and reduces administrative overhead, it also introduces challenges related to Segregation of Duties (SOD). Without proper controls, self-service IAM can lead to conflicts of interest, unauthorized privilege escalations, and compliance violations. To maintain security and regulatory compliance, organizations must integrate strong SOD policies into self-service IAM frameworks, ensuring that users cannot bypass access controls or accumulate conflicting permissions.

One of the primary benefits of self-service IAM is its ability to streamline access requests and approvals. Traditionally, access provisioning required manual intervention from IT administrators, causing delays and inefficiencies. Self-service IAM portals allow users to request access to applications, systems, and data resources through automated workflows. However, if SOD policies are not enforced, users may inadvertently or intentionally request and gain access to conflicting roles. For example, an employee in the finance department might request access to both payment processing and transaction approval systems, creating a conflict that could lead to fraud. Organizations must implement automated SOD checks within self-service IAM platforms to prevent users from requesting access that violates SOD principles.

Role-based access control (RBAC) plays a critical role in enforcing SOD within self-service IAM environments. When users request access to specific systems, RBAC policies must ensure that they only receive permissions aligned with their designated job functions. Without predefined role structures, users may receive excessive privileges, leading to security risks. Self-service IAM platforms should enforce dynamic role assignments, preventing users from gaining conflicting permissions. Additionally, organizations should implement approval workflows that require managerial or security team review for high-risk access requests, ensuring that users do not accumulate roles that violate SOD policies.

Privileged access management (PAM) is another crucial aspect of SOD enforcement in self-service IAM. Many organizations allow employees to request temporary elevated privileges through self-service IAM portals for specific administrative tasks. Without proper oversight, users could exploit this capability to gain unauthorized access to critical systems. Implementing just-in-time (JIT) privileged access, session recording, and automated expiration of elevated privileges ensures that users do not retain administrative access beyond what is necessary. Self-service IAM platforms should integrate with PAM solutions to enforce approval requirements, log all privileged activity, and prevent unauthorized privilege escalations.

Access reviews and certification processes must be automated within self-service IAM environments to maintain SOD compliance. Organizations often struggle with reviewing and revoking outdated or conflicting access rights due to manual and inefficient access governance procedures. Self-service IAM solutions should include automated access review workflows that periodically prompt managers and security teams to validate user permissions. If an SOD conflict is detected, the system should flag the violation for corrective action, such as revoking unnecessary privileges or reassigning roles. Implementing continuous access monitoring helps organizations prevent privilege accumulation and ensures that users only retain permissions necessary for their current roles.

Self-service IAM introduces security risks if users can modify their own roles or bypass approval workflows. Some self-service platforms allow users to update their job functions, reset multi-factor authentication (MFA) settings, or modify group memberships without oversight. If these modifications are not governed by SOD policies, users could manipulate their access rights to gain unauthorized permissions. Organizations must configure self-service IAM platforms to enforce strict approval workflows for role modifications and critical security settings. AI-driven anomaly detection tools can further enhance security by identifying suspicious self-service activity, such as users attempting to grant themselves unauthorized privileges.

Regulatory compliance requirements further emphasize the need for SOD enforcement in self-service IAM implementations. Organizations in finance, healthcare, and other regulated industries must adhere to standards such as the Sarbanes-Oxley Act (SOX), the General Data Protection Regulation (GDPR), and the Payment Card Industry Data Security Standard (PCI DSS). These regulations mandate strict access controls, regular access reviews, and enforcement of SOD policies to prevent financial fraud, data breaches, and insider threats. Self-service

IAM solutions should integrate with compliance tracking tools to generate audit-ready reports, ensuring that all access requests, approvals, and modifications align with regulatory requirements.

Multi-factor authentication (MFA) and risk-based authentication further strengthen SOD enforcement in self-service IAM environments. Users accessing self-service portals should be required to verify their identities using MFA before making access requests or modifying their roles. Risk-based authentication mechanisms evaluate contextual factors such as user location, device security posture, and access history to determine whether additional verification is required. If a user attempts to request high-risk access privileges, the system should enforce additional security measures, such as requiring secondary approval from a compliance officer or triggering an immediate security review.

Self-service IAM should also incorporate least privilege access principles to prevent SOD violations. Many organizations grant users broad access rights by default, increasing the risk of privilege misuse. Self-service IAM platforms should enforce the principle of least privilege by ensuring that users only request and receive the minimum permissions necessary for their tasks. Automated policy engines can evaluate each access request against predefined SOD rules, ensuring that users do not receive excessive permissions that could create conflicts of interest.

Training and awareness programs are essential to ensure that employees understand the risks associated with self-service IAM and the importance of SOD compliance. Many users may not be aware of how improper access requests can lead to security vulnerabilities, regulatory violations, or financial fraud. Organizations should conduct regular training sessions on self-service IAM best practices, secure access request procedures, and the consequences of bypassing SOD controls. Security awareness programs help reinforce compliance expectations and reduce the likelihood of unintentional SOD violations caused by improper use of self-service IAM platforms.

A well-implemented self-service IAM solution that integrates SOD controls enhances security, reduces administrative workload, and ensures regulatory compliance. By enforcing automated SOD checks, implementing approval workflows, integrating privileged access management, continuously monitoring access requests, and providing security awareness training, organizations can prevent users from acquiring conflicting roles or unauthorized privileges. Self-service IAM offers significant efficiency benefits, but without strong SOD enforcement, it can become a potential security risk. Organizations must balance automation and security by embedding robust SOD policies into self-service IAM frameworks, ensuring that users have seamless access management while maintaining strict governance and compliance standards.

Digital Transformation and the Future of SOD

Digital transformation is reshaping business operations across industries, driving automation, cloud adoption, artificial intelligence (AI), and interconnected systems that improve efficiency and agility. As organizations embrace digital transformation, the need for strong governance and security measures becomes more critical. Segregation of Duties (SOD), a foundational principle for risk management and compliance, must evolve alongside these technological advancements to remain effective. Traditional SOD models were designed for static IT environments with clearly defined roles, but in a digital-first world, organizations must rethink how they enforce SOD to prevent fraud, insider threats, and regulatory violations while enabling seamless business operations.

Cloud computing and SaaS (Software-as-a-Service) platforms have introduced new challenges for SOD enforcement. Traditional SOD frameworks were built around on-premises infrastructure, where access control was centralized within an organization's network. With cloud adoption, data and applications are distributed across multiple service providers, making it more difficult to enforce consistent SOD policies. Organizations must implement cloud identity and access management (Cloud IAM) solutions that extend SOD principles to multi-cloud environments. By leveraging role-based access control (RBAC), attribute-based access control (ABAC), and policy-based access control (PBAC), organizations can ensure that users do not accumulate conflicting privileges across different cloud services. Automated cloud security posture management (CSPM) solutions help monitor and enforce SOD policies in real time, ensuring that access violations are detected and remediated promptly.

Artificial intelligence and machine learning are revolutionizing SOD enforcement by providing real-time anomaly detection, automated access reviews, and predictive risk analysis. Traditional SOD audits were manual, reactive processes that relied on periodic reviews to identify violations. AI-driven SOD solutions continuously analyze user behavior, detect unusual access patterns, and trigger alerts when potential SOD conflicts arise. Machine learning algorithms can identify patterns in historical access data to predict which users may attempt to bypass SOD controls. By integrating AI into SOD enforcement, organizations can shift from a reactive approach to a proactive model that prevents violations before they occur.

Robotic Process Automation (RPA) is another digital transformation trend that impacts SOD enforcement. Many organizations use RPA bots to automate repetitive tasks such as financial transactions, HR processing, and supply chain management. While RPA improves efficiency, it also introduces new risks if not properly governed. If a single bot is programmed to both initiate and approve financial transactions, it violates SOD principles and creates an opportunity for fraud. Organizations must apply SOD policies to RPA by ensuring that automated processes adhere to the same role separation rules as human users. Implementing privileged access management (PAM) for RPA bots ensures that they operate within predefined limits and cannot gain unauthorized privileges.

The adoption of DevOps and Agile methodologies has transformed software development and IT operations, requiring organizations to rethink how they enforce SOD in dynamic environments. In traditional IT models, SOD was enforced by separating development, testing, and production environments, ensuring that no single individual could introduce unapproved changes. DevOps blurs these lines by promoting continuous integration and deployment (CI/CD), where developers and operations teams work collaboratively. While this accelerates software delivery, it also increases the risk of unauthorized changes and security misconfigurations. Organizations must implement DevSecOps practices that embed security and SOD controls into CI/CD pipelines. Automated code reviews, security testing, and approval workflows help ensure that no single developer has unchecked access to both development and production systems.

Identity and Access Management (IAM) is evolving to support SOD enforcement in digital environments, enabling organizations to implement real-time access controls and automated policy enforcement. Modern IAM solutions integrate with cloud platforms, SaaS applications, and on-premises systems, providing a unified approach to managing user identities and enforcing SOD policies. Adaptive authentication mechanisms enhance SOD by dynamically adjusting access privileges based on contextual risk factors such as location, device security posture, and user behavior. If an employee attempts to perform a high-risk action that conflicts with SOD policies, the IAM system can require additional authentication or trigger an approval workflow.

Blockchain technology offers new possibilities for strengthening SOD by providing immutable audit trails and decentralized access control mechanisms. In traditional SOD enforcement, audit logs are stored in centralized systems that can be modified or deleted by privileged users. Blockchain-based SOD solutions create tamper-proof access logs that ensure accountability and transparency. By using smart contracts, organizations can automate SOD policy enforcement, ensuring that conflicting actions cannot be executed without multi-party approval. Blockchain's decentralized nature also enhances third-party risk management by allowing organizations to verify vendor transactions and access history without relying on a single entity for validation.

The Internet of Things (IoT) introduces additional complexities to SOD enforcement, as connected devices generate vast amounts of data and interact with enterprise systems in real time. In industrial environments, IoT devices control critical infrastructure such as power grids, manufacturing equipment, and healthcare monitoring systems. If SOD controls are not properly implemented, a compromised IoT device could be used to manipulate operations, leading to security breaches or financial losses. Organizations must extend SOD policies to IoT environments by restricting device access to only authorized users and implementing continuous monitoring for abnormal device behavior. Integrating IoT security solutions with IAM and SIEM platforms helps detect and respond to potential violations before they impact business operations.

Regulatory compliance requirements continue to evolve alongside digital transformation, requiring organizations to adapt their SOD strategies to meet new legal and industry standards. Regulations such as the General Data Protection Regulation (GDPR), the California Consumer Privacy Act (CCPA), and the NIST Cybersecurity Framework emphasize the importance of strong access controls, continuous monitoring, and data protection. Organizations must implement automated compliance tracking tools that ensure SOD policies align with regulatory mandates. AI-driven compliance reporting solutions help generate audit-ready reports, reducing the manual effort required for regulatory audits and demonstrating adherence to security best practices.

Security awareness and employee training programs remain essential for ensuring that digital transformation initiatives do not compromise SOD enforcement. Many SOD violations occur due to human error rather than malicious intent. As employees gain access to cloud applications, remote work environments, and automated tools, they must understand how to follow SOD principles and avoid conflicts of interest. Organizations should provide regular security training that educates employees on access control best practices, privileged account security, and recognizing potential insider threats. Security champions within different business units can help reinforce SOD policies by ensuring that employees understand their responsibilities in maintaining compliance.

As digital transformation accelerates, organizations must modernize their SOD enforcement strategies to align with emerging technologies and evolving security threats. By integrating AI-driven risk analysis, automating access controls, securing cloud environments, and leveraging blockchain for audit transparency, organizations can ensure that SOD remains a foundational component of their cybersecurity and governance frameworks. The future of SOD will be defined by adaptive security models, real-time monitoring, and intelligent automation, ensuring that organizations can maintain security, compliance, and operational efficiency in an increasingly digital world.

AI-Driven Anomaly Detection in SOD

Artificial intelligence (AI) and machine learning (ML) are revolutionizing the way organizations enforce Segregation of Duties (SOD) by enabling real-time anomaly detection, automated risk assessments, and proactive threat mitigation. Traditional SOD enforcement relied on static policies, periodic audits, and manual oversight, which were often insufficient to detect complex violations or insider threats in real time. AI-driven anomaly detection enhances SOD by continuously monitoring user behavior, access patterns, and transactional activities to identify deviations that may indicate fraud, policy violations, or security risks. By leveraging AI-driven insights, organizations can strengthen their SOD frameworks, reduce compliance risks, and enhance operational integrity.

One of the key benefits of AI in SOD enforcement is its ability to analyze vast amounts of access data and detect patterns that would be impossible for human auditors to identify manually. Traditional SOD policies define clear role separations, such as ensuring that an employee who initiates a financial transaction cannot also approve it. However, in large organizations with complex workflows, access permissions evolve over time, and employees may gradually accumulate conflicting privileges. AI-driven anomaly detection continuously evaluates access logs, identifying users who have accumulated excessive privileges, circumvented SOD controls, or engaged in unauthorized actions. By proactively flagging potential violations, AI reduces the reliance on retrospective audits and helps organizations prevent risks before they materialize.

Machine learning models play a crucial role in anomaly detection by learning from historical access patterns and identifying deviations that indicate possible SOD violations. Supervised learning models are trained on known cases of policy violations, allowing them to recognize suspicious behavior with high accuracy. Unsupervised learning models, on the other hand, detect anomalies without prior knowledge of what constitutes a violation. These models analyze user activity, transaction histories, and access request patterns to identify outliers. If an employee suddenly gains access to multiple conflicting systems or exhibits behavior inconsistent with their usual workflow, AI-driven systems can trigger alerts, requiring further review before unauthorized actions are allowed to proceed.

Real-time monitoring and AI-driven threat detection are particularly valuable in preventing insider threats within SOD frameworks. Many insider threats involve employees who have legitimate access to critical systems but exploit their privileges for unauthorized activities. Traditional security measures often fail to detect gradual privilege accumulation or subtle policy violations. AI-driven solutions continuously assess user behavior, comparing it against normal baselines to detect deviations. If an employee who normally accesses payroll data suddenly attempts to modify supplier payment details, AI-driven anomaly detection can flag the activity for immediate review, preventing potential fraud or financial misconduct.

Privileged access management (PAM) is another area where AI-driven anomaly detection enhances SOD enforcement. Privileged users, such as system administrators, database managers, and finance executives, have high-level access to critical systems, making them potential targets for security breaches or insider attacks. AI-based solutions monitor privileged user sessions in real time, identifying abnormal behavior such as unauthorized privilege escalation, unusual login locations, or access attempts outside of standard working hours. By integrating AI-driven anomaly detection with PAM solutions, organizations can enforce stricter controls on privileged accounts, ensuring that no single user can bypass security policies without triggering alerts.

AI-driven anomaly detection also plays a crucial role in cloud environments, where traditional SOD enforcement mechanisms may be less effective. Cloud platforms operate in highly dynamic environments, where access permissions change frequently, and users interact with multiple cloud applications simultaneously. Static SOD policies often struggle to keep pace with these rapid changes. AI-based solutions provide adaptive risk assessments, continuously analyzing access patterns and flagging potential policy violations in real time. If a cloud user is granted excessive permissions due to misconfigured access policies, AI-driven monitoring can detect and correct the issue before it leads to a security breach.

Regulatory compliance is another area where AI-driven anomaly detection strengthens SOD enforcement. Organizations operating in highly regulated industries, such as finance, healthcare, and government, must adhere to strict access control policies to comply with regulations such as the Sarbanes-Oxley Act (SOX), the General Data Protection Regulation (GDPR), and the Payment Card Industry Data Security Standard (PCI DSS). AI-based solutions automate compliance monitoring by continuously scanning user access logs, identifying violations, and generating audit-ready reports. This reduces the burden of manual compliance reviews while ensuring that SOD policies remain effective in preventing fraud and security breaches.

AI-driven predictive analytics further enhance SOD enforcement by identifying emerging risks before they escalate into security incidents. By analyzing historical data, AI can predict which users are most likely to violate SOD policies based on behavioral trends, access patterns, and past security incidents. If an employee has a history of requesting conflicting access privileges or bypassing approval workflows, AI-driven systems can proactively restrict their access or require additional verification before granting high-risk permissions. This predictive approach enables organizations to prevent violations rather than merely responding to them after they occur.

The integration of AI-driven anomaly detection with Identity and Access Management (IAM) systems further enhances SOD enforcement by ensuring that access requests are continuously evaluated against risk-based models. When users request access to critical systems, AI algorithms assess the request against historical behavior, peer group analysis, and contextual risk factors such as device security posture and geolocation. If an access request is deemed high-risk, AI-driven IAM solutions can automatically enforce additional approval steps, multi-factor authentication (MFA), or temporary access restrictions to mitigate potential SOD violations.

Organizations must also consider the ethical and operational implications of AI-driven SOD enforcement. While AI enhances security and compliance, it is essential to ensure that AI models are transparent, unbiased, and aligned with organizational policies. Over-reliance on AI-driven anomaly detection without human oversight can lead to false positives, where legitimate activities are incorrectly flagged as violations. To address this challenge, organizations should implement a hybrid approach that combines AI-driven monitoring with human review processes. Security teams should have the ability to validate AI-generated alerts, ensuring that enforcement actions are based on accurate risk assessments.

AI-driven anomaly detection is transforming SOD enforcement by enabling real-time risk assessment, continuous monitoring, and predictive security measures. By leveraging machine learning models, organizations can detect SOD violations faster, prevent privilege escalation, and ensure compliance with regulatory requirements. Integrating AI with IAM, PAM, and compliance monitoring solutions enhances security by providing a proactive approach to risk management. As AI technology continues to evolve, organizations must refine their SOD frameworks to take full advantage of AI-driven insights while maintaining a balance between automation, transparency, and human oversight.

Blockchain Technology for SOD Enforcement

Blockchain technology has emerged as a transformative tool for enforcing Segregation of Duties (SOD) by providing immutable audit trails, decentralized access control, and automated transaction verification. Traditional SOD enforcement relies on centralized identity and access management (IAM) systems, periodic audits, and manual oversight to prevent conflicts of interest, fraud, and insider threats. However, these approaches are prone to human error, privilege escalation, and security gaps. Blockchain introduces a decentralized and tamper-proof framework for recording access control decisions, tracking privileged activities, and enforcing SOD policies without relying on a single point of failure. By leveraging blockchain technology, organizations can strengthen their SOD enforcement mechanisms, enhance regulatory compliance, and improve transparency in financial transactions, supply chain operations, and IT security.

One of the key advantages of blockchain in SOD enforcement is its ability to provide an immutable audit trail for all access and transaction-related activities. Traditional SOD models rely on centralized logs stored within IT systems, making them vulnerable to tampering by privileged users. In cases of fraud or unauthorized modifications, users with administrative access may alter or delete logs to cover their tracks. Blockchain-based audit trails eliminate this risk by recording all access events and role changes in a distributed ledger that cannot be altered or erased. Each transaction is cryptographically secured and time-stamped, ensuring that all activities remain transparent and verifiable. Organizations can use blockchain-based logging to detect and investigate SOD violations with confidence, reducing the risk of fraud and security breaches.

Smart contracts, a key feature of blockchain technology, further enhance SOD enforcement by automating access control decisions and workflow approvals. In traditional systems, access approvals are often managed through manual workflows or IAM policies that require human intervention. These processes can be slow, inconsistent, and vulnerable to manipulation. Blockchain-based smart contracts execute predefined rules autonomously, ensuring that SOD policies are enforced without human interference. For example, if an employee requests access to approve financial transactions, a smart contract can automatically verify whether the user already holds conflicting permissions. If a conflict is detected, the access request is denied, and an alert is generated. This automated enforcement mechanism ensures that SOD policies remain consistent and free from manipulation.

Blockchain enhances access control by implementing decentralized identity management, reducing the risk of privilege accumulation and unauthorized role changes. In traditional IAM systems, administrators control user roles and permissions, creating opportunities for privilege abuse or accidental access misconfigurations. Blockchain-based identity solutions, such as self-sovereign identity (SSI), provide a decentralized approach to identity management where users have cryptographic proof of their identities without relying on a central authority. Each user's access rights are stored in a blockchain ledger, preventing unauthorized modifications by IT administrators or privileged users. When a user's role changes, blockchain ensures that access modifications follow strict SOD rules, preventing users from accumulating conflicting privileges over time.

Supply chain security and financial transaction verification are other areas where blockchain improves SOD enforcement. Organizations often rely on multiple stakeholders, including suppliers, contractors, and third-party vendors, to conduct business operations. Without proper oversight, conflicting responsibilities can arise, leading to fraud or unauthorized financial transactions. Blockchain provides a decentralized and transparent method for verifying transactions, ensuring that each step in the approval process is independently validated. When an invoice is issued, for example, blockchain ensures that the payment authorization process follows SOD principles by requiring multiple approvals recorded on an immutable ledger. This prevents any single individual from having unchecked control over both invoice approval and payment execution.

Regulatory compliance is a major driver of blockchain adoption in SOD enforcement. Organizations in finance, healthcare, and government must comply with strict regulations such as the Sarbanes-Oxley Act (SOX), the General Data Protection Regulation (GDPR), and the Payment Card Industry Data Security Standard (PCI DSS). These regulations mandate strong access controls, audit trails, and fraud prevention mechanisms. Traditional compliance audits require extensive manual reviews, increasing the risk of human error and oversight. Blockchain-based compliance tracking automates regulatory reporting by ensuring that all access and transaction records are cryptographically signed, time-stamped, and immutable. Auditors can instantly verify compliance by accessing the blockchain ledger, reducing the burden of manual audits and improving transparency.

Privileged access management (PAM) benefits significantly from blockchain-based SOD enforcement by ensuring that privileged users cannot alter security controls or bypass policy restrictions. In traditional IT environments, privileged users such as system administrators and database managers have the ability to modify access logs, disable security controls, or assign themselves excessive permissions. Blockchain mitigates this risk by decentralizing control over privileged access decisions, ensuring that no single user can modify security policies without independent verification. When a privileged user attempts to make changes to critical systems, blockchain-based authentication mechanisms require multi-party consensus, preventing unauthorized privilege escalation.

AI-driven anomaly detection integrated with blockchain further strengthens SOD enforcement by identifying unusual access patterns and triggering real-time alerts. Machine learning algorithms analyze historical access data stored on the blockchain, detecting anomalies such as unexpected role changes, unauthorized privilege escalations, or high-risk financial transactions. When a deviation from normal access behavior is detected, blockchain-based security controls can automatically revoke permissions, enforce additional authentication steps, or escalate the issue for human review. This proactive approach to risk mitigation ensures that SOD policies remain effective in preventing insider threats and fraudulent activities.

Blockchain technology also plays a crucial role in preventing data tampering and ensuring data integrity in SOD enforcement. In traditional IT environments, security breaches often involve unauthorized modifications to sensitive data, leading to fraudulent activities or compliance violations. Blockchain's decentralized ledger structure ensures that all data transactions are permanently recorded and cannot be altered retroactively. If an employee attempts to manipulate financial records, payroll data, or procurement logs, blockchain technology ensures that the modification is permanently logged, making it impossible to erase or falsify transaction histories. This guarantees data integrity and provides an indisputable record of all activities for forensic investigations.

As organizations continue to adopt blockchain for SOD enforcement, they must consider scalability and integration challenges. Blockchain networks require significant computational resources, and integrating blockchain-based SOD controls with existing IAM and ERP systems can be complex. Organizations must carefully evaluate whether a private, consortium, or public blockchain model best aligns with their security and compliance needs. Private blockchains offer greater control and scalability, while public blockchains provide enhanced transparency and decentralization. Regardless of the implementation model, organizations must ensure that blockchain-based SOD enforcement aligns with their overall security, compliance, and operational strategies.

Blockchain technology is transforming SOD enforcement by providing immutable audit trails, decentralized identity management, automated policy enforcement, and real-time anomaly detection. By integrating blockchain with IAM, PAM, and compliance monitoring solutions, organizations can strengthen their security frameworks, prevent fraud, and ensure regulatory compliance. As blockchain adoption continues to grow, its role in SOD enforcement will become increasingly vital, offering a more transparent, tamper-proof, and efficient approach to managing access controls and preventing conflicts of interest in business operations.

Cloud Identity Providers and SOD Compliance

Cloud identity providers (IdPs) have become essential components of modern IT environments, enabling organizations to manage user identities, access control, and authentication across multiple cloud-based services. As businesses continue migrating workloads to the cloud, the need for strong governance and compliance measures, including Segregation of Duties (SOD), becomes increasingly critical. Traditional SOD enforcement mechanisms were designed for on-premises environments where access control was centralized. In contrast, cloud environments introduce dynamic access models, federated identities, and third-party integrations that can complicate SOD enforcement. Cloud identity providers offer a scalable solution for enforcing SOD policies across distributed systems, ensuring that users cannot accumulate conflicting permissions or bypass approval processes.

One of the fundamental roles of cloud identity providers in SOD compliance is managing identity federation across multiple cloud applications and platforms. Organizations often use a combination of

Software-as-a-Service (SaaS), Infrastructure-as-a-Service (IaaS), and Platform-as-a-Service (PaaS) solutions, each with its own access control policies. Without a centralized identity provider, managing SOD across disparate cloud services becomes challenging, increasing the risk of privilege escalation and policy violations. Cloud IdPs, such as Microsoft Entra ID, Okta, and Google Cloud Identity, provide a unified authentication layer that enforces consistent access policies across all cloud services. By integrating cloud identity providers with IAM solutions, organizations can define SOD-compliant access controls, ensuring that users do not inherit conflicting privileges across different cloud platforms.

Role-based access control (RBAC) and attribute-based access control (ABAC) are critical capabilities of cloud identity providers that help enforce SOD policies. RBAC ensures that users are assigned roles with predefined permissions based on their job functions, preventing them from acquiring conflicting access rights. ABAC further enhances SOD enforcement by considering additional attributes, such as user location, device security posture, and time of access, before granting permissions. For example, if an employee responsible for approving financial transactions attempts to request access to payment processing systems, ABAC policies can evaluate whether this access would violate SOD rules and require additional approvals before granting access. By leveraging RBAC and ABAC within cloud IdPs, organizations can prevent privilege accumulation and reduce the risk of insider threats.

Multi-factor authentication (MFA) and risk-based authentication (RBA) further strengthen SOD compliance in cloud environments by ensuring that high-risk access requests undergo additional verification. Traditional authentication mechanisms, such as passwords, are insufficient for preventing unauthorized access, especially in cloud-based environments where users access systems from multiple locations and devices. Cloud identity providers integrate MFA solutions that require users to verify their identities using biometric authentication, time-based one-time passwords (TOTP), or security keys before accessing critical systems. RBA enhances this process by analyzing contextual factors, such as user behavior, access history, and IP reputation, to determine whether an access request poses a security risk. If a cloud user attempts to access conflicting SOD-controlled systems, the cloud IdP can enforce additional security measures, such as requiring managerial approval or triggering an access review before granting permissions.

Privileged access management (PAM) is another critical aspect of SOD enforcement in cloud environments, ensuring that users with administrative privileges do not have unchecked access to sensitive systems. Cloud identity providers integrate with PAM solutions to enforce just-in-time (JIT) access, requiring privileged users to request temporary elevated permissions rather than maintaining persistent administrative access. This approach prevents privilege abuse by ensuring that no single user has continuous access to critical cloud resources. Session recording and real-time monitoring further enhance security by logging privileged user activity and detecting unauthorized actions that may indicate SOD violations. By integrating PAM with cloud identity providers, organizations can ensure that SOD policies extend to privileged accounts, reducing the risk of insider threats and compliance violations.

Cloud identity providers also play a vital role in automating access reviews and certification processes to maintain SOD compliance. Many organizations struggle with access governance due to manual and inefficient access review procedures, leading to excessive permissions and privilege accumulation. Cloud IdPs automate periodic access reviews by generating reports on user access patterns, identifying SOD conflicts, and requiring managers to certify or revoke access rights. AI-driven identity analytics further enhance this process by detecting anomalous access behavior, such as users requesting conflicting roles or attempting to bypass approval workflows. By automating access reviews, organizations can ensure that users maintain only the necessary permissions required for their roles, preventing privilege escalation and unauthorized access.

Regulatory compliance requirements further emphasize the need for SOD enforcement through cloud identity providers. Organizations in highly regulated industries, such as finance, healthcare, and government, must comply with data protection and security standards, including the General Data Protection Regulation (GDPR), the Sarbanes-Oxley Act (SOX), and the Health Insurance Portability and Accountability Act (HIPAA). These regulations require organizations to implement strict access controls, enforce SOD policies, and maintain audit trails of user activity. Cloud IdPs provide compliance tracking tools that generate audit logs, monitor access events, and enforce role separation in accordance with regulatory requirements. By integrating cloud identity providers with compliance management platforms, organizations can streamline regulatory reporting and ensure adherence to security best practices.

Zero Trust security frameworks complement SOD enforcement in cloud environments by eliminating implicit trust and continuously verifying user access. Traditional security models often assume that users inside the corporate network are trustworthy, granting them broad access to internal systems. However, as organizations adopt cloud-first strategies and enable remote work, Zero Trust principles enforce continuous authentication, least privilege access, and micro-segmentation to prevent unauthorized access. Cloud identity providers play a central role in Zero Trust architectures by enforcing adaptive access policies that evaluate user identity, device security, and contextual risk factors before granting permissions. If a user attempts to access a cloud service that conflicts with their assigned role, Zero Trust policies can trigger additional authentication steps or require explicit approvals before allowing access.

Third-party integrations with cloud identity providers introduce additional challenges for SOD compliance, as external vendors, contractors, and business partners often require access to cloud applications and sensitive data. Without proper governance, third-party users may accumulate excessive permissions, leading to security risks and compliance violations. Cloud IdPs enforce least privilege access for third-party users by implementing time-restricted access policies, requiring federated authentication, and monitoring external user activity for potential SOD violations. By implementing third-party risk management solutions alongside cloud identity providers, organizations can ensure that vendors and contractors adhere to SOD policies, reducing the risk of unauthorized access and privilege misuse.

Security training and awareness programs remain essential for ensuring that employees and administrators understand the role of cloud identity providers in SOD compliance. Many security breaches occur due to human error, such as misconfiguring access controls, sharing credentials, or approving unauthorized access requests. Organizations should conduct regular training sessions on cloud identity governance, SOD best practices, and the importance of following role-based access policies. Security awareness campaigns reinforce compliance expectations and help prevent accidental SOD violations that could lead to financial fraud, data breaches, or regulatory penalties.

Cloud identity providers are integral to modern SOD enforcement, offering centralized authentication, automated access governance, and risk-based access controls to prevent privilege accumulation and unauthorized role conflicts. By integrating cloud IdPs with IAM, PAM, Zero Trust security models, and compliance tracking solutions, organizations can enforce SOD policies across distributed cloud environments while maintaining regulatory compliance. As cloud adoption continues to grow, leveraging identity providers for SOD enforcement will become increasingly vital in securing cloud-based infrastructures, preventing insider threats, and ensuring access control integrity.

SOD in Identity Federation and Single Sign-On (SSO)

Segregation of Duties (SOD) is a fundamental principle in identity and access management (IAM) that prevents users from accumulating excessive privileges that could lead to fraud, data breaches, or unauthorized system modifications. As organizations increasingly adopt identity federation and Single Sign-On (SSO) solutions to streamline authentication and access management across multiple applications, enforcing SOD becomes more complex. Identity federation allows users to authenticate once and access multiple systems using a centralized identity provider, while SSO eliminates the need for repeated logins, enhancing user experience and operational efficiency. However, without proper SOD enforcement, these technologies can introduce security risks by enabling users to gain conflicting privileges across multiple systems. Organizations must implement robust SOD controls within identity federation and SSO frameworks to prevent privilege escalation, ensure compliance, and maintain security across distributed IT environments.

One of the primary challenges of enforcing SOD in identity federation is managing role assignments across different domains and organizations. Identity federation enables users to authenticate with an external identity provider (IdP) and gain access to multiple applications and services, often spanning different organizations or cloud environments. While this reduces the need for managing multiple credentials, it also creates the risk of privilege conflicts if users are assigned roles that violate SOD policies. For example, an employee working for a financial services provider could use federated access to gain administrative privileges in both an internal banking application and a third-party payment processing system. Without proper SOD enforcement, this could enable unauthorized fund transfers or policy circumvention. Organizations must implement role-mapping policies that restrict users from obtaining conflicting privileges across federated systems, ensuring that each user maintains access only to functions appropriate for their role.

SSO solutions further complicate SOD enforcement by centralizing authentication, potentially allowing users to bypass access controls if proper restrictions are not in place. In traditional IAM environments, users authenticate separately for each system, allowing organizations to apply granular access controls at each authentication point. With SSO, users authenticate once and gain access to multiple applications without needing to re-enter credentials, making it more challenging to enforce SOD policies dynamically. If an SSO system is misconfigured, a user who should only have approval rights in an accounting system could also gain access to initiate transactions, violating SOD principles. To mitigate this risk, organizations must implement access control policies that evaluate user roles before granting SSO-based access, ensuring that users do not inadvertently receive excessive permissions.

Federated identity providers must integrate with SOD enforcement mechanisms to prevent cross-domain privilege escalation. Many organizations use Security Assertion Markup Language (SAML), OpenID Connect (OIDC), or OAuth to enable identity federation across cloud applications and third-party services. While these protocols streamline authentication, they do not inherently enforce

SOD policies. Without proper controls, users could receive conflicting roles across different identity providers, leading to unauthorized actions. Organizations should implement federated identity governance frameworks that enforce SOD rules at the identity provider level, restricting users from receiving roles that conflict with existing access policies. This requires integrating identity federation platforms with role-based access control (RBAC) or attribute-based access control (ABAC) models to ensure that users receive consistent, policy-compliant permissions across all connected systems.

Multi-factor authentication (MFA) and risk-based authentication (RBA) play a critical role in securing SSO and identity federation while enforcing SOD policies. Since SSO provides users with seamless access to multiple applications, organizations must ensure that high-risk access requests undergo additional verification. MFA requires users to provide additional proof of identity, such as biometric authentication or time-based one-time passwords (TOTP), before accessing sensitive systems. RBA enhances this process by evaluating contextual factors, such as login location, device security posture, and previous access history, to determine whether an authentication attempt poses a risk. If a federated user attempts to access a system that conflicts with their assigned role, the identity provider can enforce step-up authentication or deny access altogether, ensuring that SOD policies remain intact.

Privileged access management (PAM) is essential for enforcing SOD within federated identity and SSO environments, particularly for users with administrative or high-level access. Many organizations grant privileged users access to multiple systems through SSO, creating a security risk if those users can escalate their privileges across federated domains. Without proper PAM integration, an administrator with SSO access to both a cloud database and a security configuration platform could bypass security controls, modify critical settings, or exfiltrate sensitive data. To prevent this, organizations should enforce just-in-time (JIT) privileged access, requiring users to request temporary elevated privileges instead of maintaining continuous high-level access. PAM solutions integrated with identity federation ensure that privileged users do not violate SOD policies by requiring multi-step approvals, real-time session monitoring, and automatic privilege expiration.

Audit logging and continuous monitoring further strengthen SOD enforcement in identity federation and SSO frameworks by providing visibility into access events and policy violations. Since SSO enables users to access multiple systems with a single authentication session, organizations must implement centralized logging to track user activity across all federated services. Security Information and Event Management (SIEM) solutions help detect anomalies, such as users accessing conflicting systems or attempting unauthorized role modifications. AI-driven analytics further enhance monitoring by identifying unusual access patterns and flagging potential SOD violations for immediate review. By continuously analyzing authentication and access events, organizations can detect privilege misuse, enforce policy compliance, and mitigate insider threats in real time.

Regulatory compliance requirements emphasize the need for enforcing SOD within identity federation and SSO environments. Many industries are subject to strict access control regulations, such as the Sarbanes-Oxley Act (SOX), the General Data Protection Regulation (GDPR), and the Health Insurance Portability and Accountability Act (HIPAA). These regulations require organizations to implement strict access controls, conduct periodic access reviews, and prevent unauthorized privilege escalation. Identity federation and SSO must align with compliance requirements by ensuring that users do not receive conflicting roles across federated domains, access reviews are automated, and authentication logs are stored securely for audit purposes. By integrating SOD controls into federated identity management, organizations can maintain regulatory compliance while benefiting from seamless access management.

Security awareness and training programs further support SOD enforcement by educating employees, administrators, and IT security teams on the risks associated with identity federation and SSO. Many SOD violations occur due to misconfigurations, lack of oversight, or user negligence. Organizations should conduct regular training sessions on secure authentication practices, role-based access management, and recognizing privilege conflicts within federated environments. Security teams should receive specialized training on configuring identity federation platforms to enforce SOD policies, ensuring that misconfigurations do not lead to security breaches or compliance failures.

Identity federation and SSO provide significant advantages in simplifying authentication and access management, but they also introduce new challenges for enforcing SOD. By integrating RBAC and ABAC, leveraging MFA and risk-based authentication, implementing privileged access management, continuously monitoring authentication events, and ensuring regulatory compliance, organizations can enforce SOD policies while maintaining security and efficiency in federated identity environments. As organizations continue adopting cloud-first strategies and multi-domain authentication models, robust SOD enforcement within identity federation and SSO will remain essential for preventing unauthorized access, privilege escalation, and security threats.

SOD in Remote Work and BYOD Environments

The rise of remote work and Bring Your Own Device (BYOD) policies has transformed how organizations manage access control, authentication, and security governance. While these flexible work arrangements improve productivity and employee satisfaction, they introduce significant challenges in enforcing Segregation of Duties (SOD). Traditionally, SOD policies were easier to enforce in centralized office environments, where access to critical systems was restricted to corporate networks and company-managed devices. In remote work and BYOD environments, users access corporate applications from various locations and personal devices, increasing the risk of unauthorized access, privilege accumulation, and insider threats. To maintain compliance and security, organizations must implement robust SOD controls that account for the complexities of remote access, cloud-based applications, and unmanaged endpoints.

One of the key challenges in enforcing SOD in remote work environments is the lack of physical oversight and direct control over user access. In an office setting, access to sensitive systems can be restricted through network segmentation, physical security controls, and on-site monitoring. With remote work, employees connect to corporate systems through virtual private networks (VPNs), cloud applications, and remote desktop solutions. Without proper access restrictions, employees could gain excessive privileges that violate SOD policies, such as the ability to both initiate and approve financial transactions. Organizations must implement strict role-based access control (RBAC) and attribute-based access control (ABAC) models to ensure that users can only perform tasks aligned with their job functions, regardless of their location or device.

Multi-factor authentication (MFA) is essential for enforcing SOD in remote work and BYOD environments. Since remote employees access corporate systems from various networks, including home Wi-Fi and public hotspots, authentication mechanisms must verify user identities beyond just passwords. MFA requires additional authentication factors, such as biometric recognition, security tokens, or time-based one-time passwords (TOTP), before granting access to critical systems. This ensures that even if a remote employee's credentials are compromised, attackers cannot easily exploit them to bypass SOD policies. Risk-based authentication further strengthens security by evaluating contextual factors such as device trustworthiness, geolocation, and user behavior to determine whether additional verification is required.

Cloud identity providers (IdPs) play a crucial role in enforcing SOD in remote and BYOD environments by providing centralized access control across multiple cloud services. Traditional access control models were designed for on-premises applications, where IT administrators had full control over authentication policies. In remote work settings, employees use cloud-based collaboration tools, virtual desktops, and SaaS applications that may be outside the direct control of corporate IT. Without a centralized identity provider, users may accumulate conflicting privileges across different cloud services. Integrating SOD policies into cloud IAM solutions ensures that remote employees cannot inadvertently obtain access rights that violate SOD principles. Identity federation and single sign-on (SSO) solutions further streamline access management while enforcing least privilege access.

Privileged access management (PAM) is critical in remote work environments, where IT administrators, developers, and security teams often require elevated privileges to perform system maintenance, troubleshoot issues, or deploy updates. Without proper oversight, remote privileged users may escalate their own access, modify security configurations, or bypass SOD policies. Organizations should implement just-in-time (JIT) privileged access controls, ensuring that remote users receive temporary administrative privileges only when necessary. Session recording and real-time monitoring provide additional security by tracking privileged activities and detecting unauthorized actions. Automated approval workflows should be enforced to ensure that no single remote employee can execute conflicting administrative tasks without independent oversight.

Endpoint security plays a vital role in enforcing SOD in BYOD environments, where employees use personal laptops, tablets, and smartphones to access corporate applications. Unlike company-managed devices, personal devices may not have enterprise-grade security controls, increasing the risk of malware infections, data breaches, and unauthorized access. Organizations must implement endpoint detection and response (EDR) solutions to monitor device health, enforce security policies, and prevent unauthorized software installations. Zero Trust security models further enhance SOD enforcement by requiring continuous verification of device compliance before granting access to sensitive systems. If a BYOD device does not meet security requirements, access should be restricted, and remediation steps should be enforced before allowing entry to corporate applications.

Remote work also introduces new risks related to data access and document management. Employees working from home or public locations may store sensitive files on personal devices, upload corporate documents to unauthorized cloud storage services, or share confidential information through unapproved communication channels. These practices can create SOD conflicts if unauthorized users gain access to financial records, customer data, or intellectual property. Organizations should enforce data loss prevention (DLP) policies that restrict file transfers, prevent unauthorized data sharing, and encrypt sensitive documents. Secure collaboration platforms with built-in access controls help ensure that remote employees can only access and modify data within their assigned permissions, reducing the risk of policy violations.

Regular access reviews and certification processes are essential to maintain SOD compliance in remote work and BYOD environments. Since employees may change roles, switch devices, or gain additional access over time, organizations must periodically review user privileges to ensure they align with SOD policies. Automated access review workflows streamline this process by generating reports on user permissions, detecting conflicting roles, and requiring managers to certify access rights. AI-driven identity analytics further enhance this process by identifying anomalous access patterns, such as employees attempting to access systems outside their designated job functions. By continuously reviewing and revoking unnecessary privileges, organizations can prevent SOD violations and reduce the risk of privilege accumulation.

Regulatory compliance requirements emphasize the importance of SOD enforcement in remote work environments, particularly for organizations operating in finance, healthcare, and government sectors. Regulations such as the General Data Protection Regulation (GDPR), the Sarbanes-Oxley Act (SOX), and the Health Insurance Portability and Accountability Act (HIPAA) require strict access controls, secure authentication mechanisms, and periodic security audits. Remote work and BYOD policies must align with these compliance requirements by ensuring that employees do not have conflicting privileges that could lead to financial fraud, data breaches, or regulatory violations. Compliance automation tools help organizations track user access, enforce policy controls, and generate audit-ready reports for regulatory assessments.

Security awareness and training programs play a crucial role in enforcing SOD in remote work environments. Many security incidents occur due to human error, such as employees sharing passwords, using weak authentication methods, or bypassing security controls. Organizations should provide regular training on secure remote access practices, the risks associated with privilege escalation, and the importance of following SOD policies. Remote employees should also be trained on recognizing phishing attempts, avoiding insecure Wi-Fi networks, and using company-approved security tools. By fostering a security-conscious culture, organizations can reduce the likelihood of SOD violations and improve overall compliance with access control policies.

Remote work and BYOD policies introduce new complexities in enforcing SOD, requiring organizations to adapt their access control strategies to dynamic and distributed work environments. By leveraging cloud identity providers, multi-factor authentication, privileged access management, endpoint security, and continuous monitoring, organizations can ensure that remote employees and BYOD users adhere to SOD policies while maintaining security and compliance. As organizations continue to embrace flexible work models, enforcing SOD in remote work and BYOD environments will remain a critical component of cybersecurity and risk management strategies.

SOD Metrics and Reporting

Segregation of Duties (SOD) is a critical component of risk management, fraud prevention, and regulatory compliance. However, the effectiveness of SOD policies depends on the ability of organizations to measure their enforcement, identify violations, and generate actionable insights. SOD metrics and reporting provide organizations with a structured approach to monitor access control, detect policy violations, and ensure that controls remain effective over time. Without proper metrics and reporting mechanisms, organizations risk allowing privilege accumulation, unauthorized access, and compliance failures to go undetected. Establishing a robust system for tracking SOD violations, analyzing risk exposure, and generating audit-ready reports is essential for maintaining security and operational integrity.

One of the key aspects of SOD metrics is tracking the number and severity of SOD conflicts across an organization. Organizations must regularly assess how many users have conflicting roles, such as the ability to both initiate and approve financial transactions or modify system settings without oversight. A high number of SOD conflicts may indicate weak access control policies, excessive privilege accumulation, or misconfigured role assignments. By categorizing conflicts based on their severity, organizations can prioritize remediation efforts and ensure that high-risk conflicts are resolved before they lead to security incidents. Tracking these metrics over time also helps organizations evaluate the effectiveness of their SOD policies and make necessary adjustments.

Monitoring access request trends is another important metric in SOD enforcement. Organizations must analyze the volume of access requests submitted, approved, and denied within a given period to identify patterns that may indicate policy violations. If a significant number of access requests are being approved without proper review, it may suggest that SOD controls are not being enforced consistently. Conversely, if access requests are frequently denied due to SOD conflicts, it may indicate that employees are not aware of access control policies or that role assignments need to be refined. By analyzing access request trends, organizations can identify gaps in policy enforcement and improve the efficiency of their identity governance processes.

SOD exception management is a critical area for reporting and analysis. In some cases, organizations must grant temporary exceptions to SOD policies due to urgent business needs or resource limitations. However, granting exceptions without proper oversight can introduce security risks. Organizations should track the number of SOD exceptions granted, the reasons for the exceptions, and the duration of the exceptions. If exceptions become frequent, it may indicate that SOD policies are too restrictive or misaligned with business processes. Automated exception tracking ensures that all deviations from SOD policies are documented, reviewed, and approved by authorized personnel, reducing the risk of privilege misuse.

User access reviews play a vital role in ensuring that SOD policies remain effective over time. Organizations must conduct periodic reviews to verify that employees, contractors, and third-party users have appropriate access based on their job functions. Metrics related to access reviews include the percentage of users whose access was modified or revoked, the number of unresolved access conflicts, and the average time taken to complete reviews. A high percentage of revoked access may indicate that users are retaining privileges longer than necessary, while a low completion rate for access reviews may suggest inefficiencies in the review process. Automating access reviews through identity governance solutions helps organizations maintain compliance with SOD policies and reduce the risk of privilege accumulation.

SOD violation detection and response time are crucial metrics for assessing the organization's ability to identify and mitigate policy breaches. Organizations should track the time taken to detect SOD violations, investigate incidents, and implement corrective actions. A prolonged response time may indicate inefficiencies in security monitoring or a lack of automated enforcement mechanisms. Implementing AI-driven anomaly detection and real-time access monitoring helps organizations reduce response times by detecting policy violations as they occur and triggering automated alerts. Rapid detection and remediation of SOD violations minimize the risk of fraud, insider threats, and compliance failures.

Regulatory compliance reporting is an essential function of SOD metrics and reporting. Organizations operating in regulated industries must demonstrate compliance with laws and standards such as the Sarbanes-Oxley Act (SOX), the General Data Protection Regulation (GDPR), and the Payment Card Industry Data Security Standard (PCI DSS). Compliance-related SOD metrics include the number of audit findings related to access control, the percentage of users with excessive privileges, and the frequency of compliance assessments. Organizations must generate detailed reports that document their SOD enforcement practices, risk mitigation strategies, and corrective actions taken in response to audit findings. Automating compliance reporting ensures that organizations can quickly provide regulators with evidence of SOD compliance and reduce the risk of financial penalties.

Privileged access management (PAM) integration enhances SOD reporting by providing visibility into high-risk user activities. Privileged users, such as IT administrators and finance executives, often have elevated access that requires stricter oversight. Organizations should track metrics related to privileged session activity, unauthorized privilege escalations, and the use of just-in-time (JIT) access controls. Monitoring privileged access trends helps organizations detect unusual behavior, enforce SOD policies, and prevent unauthorized system modifications. PAM solutions with built-in reporting capabilities provide real-time insights into privileged user activities and generate audit logs for security investigations.

Cloud-based SOD enforcement introduces additional challenges for reporting and metrics. Organizations must ensure that SOD policies are consistently applied across on-premises and cloud environments. Cloud identity providers and SaaS applications generate vast amounts of access data, making it difficult to track SOD violations manually. Organizations should implement cloud security posture management (CSPM) solutions to aggregate SOD-related metrics across multiple cloud platforms. Cloud SOD reporting should include metrics such as the number of cross-cloud access conflicts, unauthorized privilege escalations in cloud environments, and the effectiveness of cloud-based identity governance policies. Standardizing SOD metrics across hybrid IT environments ensures that organizations maintain comprehensive visibility into access control risks.

Security awareness and training impact SOD enforcement effectiveness, and organizations should track metrics related to employee compliance with access control policies. Training-related SOD metrics include the percentage of employees who have completed security awareness programs, the frequency of policy violations by trained versus untrained employees, and the effectiveness of training in reducing access-related security incidents. If trained employees continue to violate SOD policies, it may indicate that training programs need improvement or that policy enforcement mechanisms are not stringent enough. Ongoing training ensures that employees understand the importance of SOD compliance and follow best practices for access management.

A robust SOD metrics and reporting framework helps organizations detect policy violations, enforce access control policies, and ensure compliance with regulatory requirements. By continuously monitoring access conflicts, tracking user access trends, automating exception management, and integrating AI-driven security analytics, organizations can proactively mitigate risks and strengthen their identity governance strategies. Standardized reporting and automated compliance tracking further enhance security by providing real-time visibility into SOD enforcement across on-premises, cloud, and hybrid environments. As organizations continue to evolve their access management practices, leveraging advanced SOD metrics and reporting capabilities will remain essential for maintaining operational integrity, preventing fraud, and meeting regulatory obligations.

Best Practices for Training and Awareness on SOD Policies

Training and awareness programs are essential for ensuring the effective implementation and enforcement of Segregation of Duties (SOD) policies within an organization. While technical controls, automated enforcement, and access management solutions help prevent SOD violations, employee awareness plays a crucial role in maintaining compliance and reducing security risks. Without proper training, employees may inadvertently violate SOD policies, leading to fraud, data breaches, and regulatory non-compliance. Establishing a structured training program that educates employees, IT teams, and management on the importance of SOD ensures that everyone understands their roles in enforcing access control policies and mitigating security risks.

One of the key elements of SOD training is defining the purpose and significance of SOD policies. Employees must understand that SOD is not just a bureaucratic requirement but a fundamental security principle designed to prevent conflicts of interest, fraud, and unauthorized access. Training should emphasize how SOD controls protect financial integrity, safeguard sensitive data, and ensure compliance with regulations such as the Sarbanes-Oxley Act (SOX), the General Data Protection Regulation (GDPR), and the Payment Card Industry Data Security Standard (PCI DSS). By linking SOD policies to real-world risks, employees gain a deeper understanding of why these controls are necessary and how they contribute to the overall security posture of the organization.

Effective SOD training programs should be role-based, ensuring that employees receive relevant information based on their job responsibilities. Different departments interact with SOD policies in unique ways, and generic training may not be sufficient to address specific risks associated with different roles. Finance teams should receive training on preventing fraudulent transactions by adhering to SOD requirements in payment processing and approval workflows. IT administrators should be educated on privileged access management (PAM) and how excessive administrative privileges can lead to security vulnerabilities. Human resources teams should understand how SOD policies apply to employee onboarding, access provisioning, and role transitions. By tailoring training content to different roles, organizations ensure that employees receive practical, applicable knowledge that aligns with their daily responsibilities.

Scenario-based training is a highly effective method for increasing awareness of SOD policies. Instead of relying solely on theoretical explanations, organizations should incorporate real-life case studies and simulated exercises that illustrate the consequences of SOD violations. Employees should be presented with hypothetical scenarios where SOD conflicts arise, such as an employee requesting access to both vendor payment processing and approval functions. Interactive training modules can prompt employees to make decisions on whether to grant or deny access, helping them develop critical thinking skills related to SOD enforcement. Analyzing real-world incidents, such as fraud cases resulting from weak SOD controls, reinforces the importance of strict adherence to SOD policies.

Periodic reinforcement of SOD training is necessary to ensure continuous awareness and prevent knowledge gaps. A one-time training session during employee onboarding is not sufficient to maintain long-term compliance. Organizations should implement recurring training sessions, refresher courses, and ongoing awareness campaigns to reinforce SOD principles. Quarterly or annual training sessions should provide updates on changes to SOD policies, emerging security threats, and best practices for maintaining compliance. Short training videos, newsletters, and interactive quizzes can be used to keep employees engaged and informed about SOD requirements.

Executive leadership support is crucial for fostering a culture of security awareness and ensuring that SOD training is taken seriously. When senior executives actively participate in SOD training programs and communicate the importance of access control policies, employees are more likely to follow best practices. Management should reinforce the message that SOD is a shared responsibility and that adherence to policies is critical for protecting the organization's assets. Establishing a compliance-driven culture where employees feel accountable for security helps strengthen SOD enforcement across all levels of the organization.

A clear reporting and escalation process should be included in SOD training programs to ensure that employees know how to identify and report potential violations. Employees may encounter situations where they suspect that a colleague has accumulated conflicting privileges or where an access control policy is being bypassed. Training should educate employees on how to recognize warning signs of SOD violations and the proper channels for reporting concerns. Organizations should establish a confidential reporting mechanism, such as an internal hotline or anonymous reporting system, to encourage employees to report potential risks without fear of retaliation. Clear escalation procedures ensure that reported concerns are promptly investigated and resolved.

Technology-based training tools, such as learning management systems (LMS), interactive e-learning modules, and gamified security awareness programs, enhance engagement and knowledge retention. Online training platforms allow organizations to track employee participation, assess knowledge retention through quizzes and assessments, and provide personalized training recommendations based on performance. Gamified training approaches, such as competitive security awareness challenges and leaderboards, make SOD training more engaging and encourage employees to actively participate in learning activities.

Testing and validation of SOD knowledge should be integrated into training programs to measure effectiveness. Organizations should conduct periodic assessments, security audits, and simulated access request scenarios to evaluate whether employees correctly apply SOD principles in their decision-making. Training programs should include post-training assessments that test employees' understanding of key concepts, such as identifying conflicting roles, approving access requests in compliance with SOD policies, and recognizing potential fraud risks. If employees consistently fail to demonstrate an understanding of SOD principles, additional training sessions and one-on-one coaching may be necessary.

Cross-departmental collaboration enhances the effectiveness of SOD training by ensuring that policies are consistently applied across all business units. The IT department, human resources, compliance teams, and finance departments should work together to develop and deliver SOD training programs. Regular meetings between these teams can help identify emerging risks, share best practices, and update training materials based on evolving security and compliance requirements. Collaborative training sessions that include representatives from different departments help reinforce the importance of cross-functional cooperation in enforcing SOD policies.

Measuring the impact of SOD training programs is essential for continuous improvement. Organizations should track key performance indicators (KPIs) related to training effectiveness, such as employee participation rates, policy adherence rates, the number of reported SOD violations, and improvements in access control audit results. Analyzing these metrics helps organizations identify gaps in training effectiveness and make data-driven decisions to enhance future training initiatives. If certain departments or teams demonstrate higher rates of SOD violations, targeted training interventions can be implemented to address specific areas of concern.

By implementing structured, role-based, and continuously reinforced SOD training programs, organizations can strengthen awareness, reduce security risks, and improve compliance with access control policies. Employees who understand SOD principles and recognize their importance are more likely to follow best practices, report potential violations, and contribute to a secure organizational environment. Establishing a culture of compliance, leveraging technology-driven training tools, and continuously monitoring training effectiveness ensures that SOD policies remain a fundamental part of an organization's risk management and security strategy.

Future Trends in IAM and SOD Policies

Identity and Access Management (IAM) and Segregation of Duties (SOD) policies are continuously evolving in response to new security threats, regulatory changes, and technological advancements. Organizations must adapt to emerging trends to maintain compliance, prevent fraud, and strengthen security frameworks. As digital transformation accelerates, IAM and SOD enforcement will become more automated, intelligent, and integrated with emerging security paradigms. The future of IAM and SOD policies will be shaped by advancements in artificial intelligence (AI), zero trust security models, decentralized identity management, and automation-driven access governance. These trends will redefine how organizations implement and enforce SOD policies while balancing security, efficiency, and user experience.

AI-driven identity governance is becoming a critical factor in the evolution of IAM and SOD policies. Traditional IAM systems rely on predefined role-based access control (RBAC) and periodic access reviews to enforce SOD. However, these methods often fail to detect evolving threats and privilege misuse in real-time. AI-powered identity analytics enhance SOD enforcement by continuously monitoring user behavior, detecting anomalies, and predicting potential violations before they occur. Machine learning models analyze historical access patterns and flag users who attempt to request or gain conflicting privileges. By integrating AI-driven risk assessments into IAM systems, organizations can implement dynamic access controls that adapt to changing risk levels and ensure real-time SOD compliance.

Zero Trust security frameworks are reshaping the way IAM and SOD policies are enforced. Traditional security models operate on the assumption that users within the corporate network are trustworthy. However, as cyber threats become more sophisticated and remote work environments expand, organizations are adopting Zero Trust principles, which require continuous identity verification and least privilege access enforcement. Zero Trust IAM ensures that users must authenticate and revalidate their access rights every time they request resources, reducing the risk of privilege accumulation. Organizations implementing Zero Trust security models will enforce SOD dynamically, using contextual risk factors such as device security posture, geolocation, and historical access behavior to determine whether access should be granted or denied.

Decentralized identity and blockchain-based access management are gaining traction as alternatives to traditional IAM frameworks. Organizations are exploring decentralized identity models that give users control over their digital identities without relying on a centralized identity provider. Blockchain technology enhances SOD enforcement by providing immutable, tamper-proof access logs that ensure accountability and transparency. Smart contracts can automate SOD policy enforcement, preventing users from performing conflicting actions without independent approvals. Decentralized identity management also strengthens third-party risk governance by ensuring that external vendors and contractors follow SOD policies without requiring direct integration with internal IAM systems. As organizations adopt blockchain for IAM, SOD policies will become more transparent, automated, and resistant to manipulation.

Identity-as-a-Service (IDaaS) solutions are becoming the standard for cloud-based IAM, offering organizations the ability to centralize identity management across multiple cloud environments. IDaaS platforms provide built-in SOD enforcement mechanisms, automated access reviews, and AI-driven policy recommendations. As multi-cloud and hybrid cloud adoption increases, organizations will rely on IDaaS to enforce SOD policies consistently across distributed IT ecosystems. These platforms integrate with SaaS applications, infrastructure services, and on-premises systems, ensuring that users do not gain conflicting privileges across different environments. The shift toward cloud-native IAM solutions will accelerate the automation of SOD enforcement, reducing the need for manual access control reviews and improving compliance with regulatory requirements.

Automated identity lifecycle management is becoming a key focus in IAM and SOD policies. Many organizations still rely on manual processes to provision, modify, and revoke user access, leading to privilege accumulation and compliance gaps. Future IAM solutions will automate identity lifecycle management using AI-driven workflows that dynamically adjust user permissions based on role changes, project assignments, and security risks. Automated access provisioning will ensure that new employees receive appropriate access without conflicting privileges, while AI-driven deprovisioning will revoke unnecessary access when users change roles or leave the organization. This approach reduces the risk of SOD violations by ensuring that user privileges remain aligned with business needs and security policies at all times.

Risk-based authentication and adaptive access control will play an increasingly important role in enforcing SOD policies. Static access policies are insufficient for detecting and mitigating modern security threats. Organizations will implement adaptive authentication mechanisms that evaluate risk factors such as login behavior, device integrity, and access history before granting privileges. If a user attempts to access a system that violates SOD policies, risk-based authentication will require additional verification, such as multi-factor authentication (MFA) or supervisor approval. AI-powered adaptive access control will ensure that SOD enforcement remains dynamic, adjusting to real-time security conditions rather than relying on fixed access control rules.

Privileged Access Management (PAM) is evolving to incorporate zero trust principles and just-in-time (JIT) access provisioning. Privileged users, such as IT administrators and security professionals, pose a higher risk due to their elevated permissions. Traditional PAM solutions enforce SOD by restricting privileged access, but future PAM implementations will incorporate AI-driven analytics to monitor privileged user activity in real time. JIT access provisioning will replace static privileged roles, ensuring that users receive administrative permissions only for the duration of a specific task. This approach prevents excessive privilege accumulation and strengthens SOD enforcement by ensuring that no single user retains continuous access to critical systems.

Regulatory compliance frameworks are becoming more stringent, requiring organizations to enhance IAM and SOD enforcement strategies. As data privacy laws continue to evolve, organizations must implement stricter access controls, continuous monitoring, and automated reporting to meet compliance standards. Future IAM solutions will integrate with compliance automation tools, providing organizations with real-time compliance dashboards and audit-ready reports. AI-driven compliance tracking will ensure that SOD policies align with industry regulations, reducing the risk of financial penalties and reputational damage. Organizations that proactively align their IAM and SOD policies with emerging regulatory requirements will be better positioned to navigate compliance challenges in an increasingly complex legal landscape.

Security awareness and IAM training will remain a critical component of SOD enforcement. Despite technological advancements, human error remains one of the leading causes of security breaches and compliance failures. Organizations will invest in continuous IAM training programs that educate employees, IT teams, and executives on the importance of SOD policies. Gamified training platforms, AI-driven security awareness programs, and interactive learning modules will improve employee engagement and knowledge retention. Organizations that prioritize security education will reduce the risk of accidental SOD violations and ensure that employees understand their responsibilities in maintaining IAM compliance.

The future of IAM and SOD policies will be defined by automation, AI-driven decision-making, decentralized identity models, and zero trust security principles. Organizations that embrace these trends will strengthen their security posture, enhance regulatory compliance, and prevent unauthorized privilege escalation. As cyber threats evolve, IAM and SOD policies must adapt to ensure that organizations remain resilient against insider threats, fraud, and access control failures. By leveraging emerging technologies and adopting proactive security strategies, organizations will continue to refine their IAM and SOD enforcement practices, ensuring robust access governance and long-term security resilience.

Challenges in Scaling SOD in Large Enterprises

Segregation of Duties (SOD) is a fundamental security and compliance principle that prevents individuals from holding conflicting roles that could lead to fraud, security breaches, or financial mismanagement. While implementing SOD in small and medium-sized businesses can be relatively straightforward, large enterprises face unique challenges in scaling SOD policies across global operations, complex IT environments, and multi-layered business structures. As organizations expand, enforcing SOD at scale becomes more difficult due to the increasing number of users, applications, third-party integrations, and regulatory requirements. Addressing these challenges requires a strategic approach that combines automation, continuous monitoring, and standardized governance frameworks.

One of the primary challenges in scaling SOD in large enterprises is the sheer volume of users and access requests. Unlike smaller organizations, where access control can be managed manually, enterprises must oversee thousands or even millions of employees, contractors, and third-party vendors. Managing SOD for such a large user base requires automated identity governance solutions that can efficiently process access requests, detect policy violations, and enforce corrective actions in real time. Without automation, security teams struggle to keep up with the high number of access changes, increasing the risk of privilege accumulation and policy violations.

Another major challenge is the complexity of enterprise IT environments. Large organizations typically operate hybrid IT infrastructures that include on-premises systems, multi-cloud platforms, legacy applications, and modern SaaS solutions. Enforcing SOD across these disparate environments requires consistent access control policies and centralized identity management frameworks. However, many enterprises still rely on siloed IAM solutions that lack interoperability, making it difficult to enforce uniform SOD policies across all systems. Integrating identity and access management (IAM) platforms with cloud identity providers, on-premises directories, and third-party authentication services is essential for ensuring that SOD policies remain effective at scale.

Role-based access control (RBAC) becomes increasingly difficult to manage as enterprises grow. In smaller organizations, defining and maintaining RBAC roles is relatively simple, with a limited number of job functions and system permissions. In contrast, large enterprises often have thousands of distinct roles, each with varying levels of access to critical business applications. Managing role hierarchies, ensuring that users do not accumulate conflicting permissions, and regularly reviewing access entitlements require significant administrative effort. Organizations must implement automated role mining and role engineering processes to streamline RBAC management and prevent excessive privilege assignments. AI-driven access analytics can help detect overlapping roles, optimize access permissions, and reduce the risk of SOD violations.

Privileged access management (PAM) presents additional challenges when scaling SOD policies. Large enterprises have a high number of privileged users, including IT administrators, security teams, and finance executives, who require elevated access to perform critical tasks. Without strict oversight, privileged users can override security controls, modify financial records, or escalate their own permissions without detection. Implementing just-in-time (JIT) privileged access controls, requiring multi-factor authentication (MFA), and enforcing real-time session monitoring help mitigate the risk of privileged SOD violations. Enterprises must also integrate PAM with IAM and security information and event management (SIEM) solutions to gain visibility into privileged user activity and detect suspicious access patterns.

Mergers and acquisitions (M&A) create significant challenges in scaling SOD policies. When enterprises merge or acquire new business units, they must integrate disparate IAM systems, align access control policies, and reconcile conflicting SOD rules. The transition period following an M&A often results in users retaining duplicate access rights across multiple systems, increasing the risk of policy violations. Organizations must conduct comprehensive access audits, identify redundant privileges, and enforce consistent SOD policies across all newly integrated entities. Automating access reconciliation processes and implementing cross-system identity federation solutions can streamline SOD enforcement during M&A transitions.

Regulatory compliance further complicates SOD enforcement in large enterprises, especially those operating across multiple jurisdictions with varying legal requirements. Enterprises must comply with industry regulations such as the Sarbanes-Oxley Act (SOX), the General Data Protection Regulation (GDPR), the Payment Card Industry Data Security Standard (PCI DSS), and other regional data protection laws. Each of these regulations imposes specific access control requirements that must be aligned with SOD policies. Ensuring compliance at scale requires centralized compliance tracking, automated audit reporting, and continuous monitoring of access control activities. Enterprises must also be prepared for regulatory audits, which require maintaining detailed records of access reviews, policy exceptions, and corrective actions taken to resolve SOD conflicts.

The expansion of remote work and bring-your-own-device (BYOD) policies further complicates SOD enforcement in large enterprises. Employees accessing corporate systems from remote locations introduce additional security risks, as IT teams have less control over network access and endpoint security. Cloud-based IAM solutions with adaptive authentication, risk-based access control, and endpoint security integrations help mitigate these risks by dynamically adjusting user permissions based on real-time risk assessments. Organizations must ensure that remote employees and third-party vendors do not bypass SOD policies by accessing sensitive systems from unmanaged devices or unsecured networks.

Continuous monitoring and real-time threat detection are essential for maintaining SOD compliance at scale. Traditional access reviews and periodic audits are no longer sufficient for detecting sophisticated insider threats and privilege misuse. Large enterprises must deploy AI-driven anomaly detection tools that continuously analyze user behavior, detect access pattern deviations, and flag potential SOD violations. Integrating machine learning models with SIEM platforms enhances security by providing automated alerts and risk-based scoring of access activities. By leveraging real-time analytics, enterprises can proactively identify and remediate SOD violations before they escalate into security incidents.

Change management and employee training are critical components of scaling SOD policies in large enterprises. As organizations evolve, employees frequently change roles, take on new responsibilities, or transition between departments. Without proper access controls in place, these transitions can lead to unintended privilege accumulation and SOD conflicts. Organizations must establish formalized access review processes, conduct periodic role revalidations, and implement automated role reassignment workflows to prevent unauthorized access. Additionally, employees must be educated on the importance of SOD policies through ongoing security awareness training. Training programs should include real-world examples of SOD violations, best practices for secure access management, and guidelines for reporting potential policy breaches.

Large enterprises must also address the challenge of managing third-party access while enforcing SOD policies. Contractors, consultants, suppliers, and business partners often require access to internal systems, but granting excessive privileges to external users increases security risks. Organizations must implement third-party risk management strategies that include time-restricted access controls, federated identity authentication, and automated privilege revocation upon contract termination. Integrating vendor risk assessment tools with IAM solutions helps ensure that third-party users do not gain conflicting access rights that could compromise enterprise security.

Scaling SOD policies in large enterprises requires a combination of automation, AI-driven analytics, centralized identity governance, and continuous monitoring. Organizations must adopt advanced IAM solutions that integrate seamlessly across hybrid and multi-cloud environments, ensuring consistent access control enforcement. By leveraging automated compliance tracking, AI-powered risk detection, and adaptive authentication mechanisms, enterprises can effectively manage SOD at scale while maintaining security, compliance, and operational efficiency. Addressing these challenges proactively ensures that large enterprises can protect their critical assets, prevent insider threats, and meet regulatory requirements in an increasingly complex digital landscape.

The Road Ahead for SOD in IAM

Segregation of Duties (SOD) has long been a cornerstone of risk management, access control, and regulatory compliance in Identity and Access Management (IAM). As organizations navigate an increasingly complex digital landscape, the role of SOD continues to evolve in response to technological advancements, emerging security threats, and shifting regulatory frameworks. The future of SOD in IAM will be defined by a convergence of automation, artificial intelligence

(AI), cloud-based identity solutions, and adaptive security models. Organizations must proactively refine their SOD enforcement strategies to ensure that access governance remains effective, scalable, and resilient against modern cybersecurity challenges.

One of the most significant developments shaping the future of SOD is the rapid adoption of AI-driven identity governance. Traditional SOD enforcement relied on predefined role-based access control (RBAC) frameworks, static access policies, and periodic audits to detect policy violations. However, these methods often fall short in identifying real-time threats and insider risks. AI-powered IAM solutions are transforming SOD enforcement by continuously analyzing access patterns, detecting anomalies, and predicting potential violations before they occur. Machine learning algorithms can assess historical access data, identify users with excessive privileges, and automatically recommend corrective actions. As organizations integrate AI-driven access analytics into their IAM strategies, SOD enforcement will become more dynamic, reducing reliance on manual reviews and improving risk mitigation.

The rise of Zero Trust security models is also redefining how organizations implement and enforce SOD policies. Traditional perimeter-based security approaches assumed that users within an organization's network could be trusted. However, as remote work, cloud adoption, and third-party integrations expand, Zero Trust principles demand continuous authentication, least privilege access, and micro-segmentation of resources. SOD policies will need to align with Zero Trust by enforcing real-time access decisions based on contextual risk factors such as user behavior, device health, and geolocation. Organizations must integrate SOD enforcement with Zero Trust architectures to ensure that users cannot bypass policy restrictions, even when accessing cloud-based applications or remote resources.

Cloud identity providers (IdPs) and Identity-as-a-Service (IDaaS) platforms are playing an increasingly central role in managing SOD policies across multi-cloud and hybrid IT environments. As organizations migrate workloads to the cloud, ensuring consistent SOD enforcement across SaaS, IaaS, and PaaS ecosystems becomes more challenging. Cloud IdPs offer centralized authentication, federated access management, and policy-based access controls that help organizations maintain SOD compliance across distributed environments. Future advancements in IDaaS will further enhance SOD enforcement by integrating automated access reviews, real-time risk assessments, and AI-driven policy recommendations. Organizations must leverage cloud-native IAM solutions to streamline SOD governance while maintaining security and compliance in evolving cloud ecosystems.

The automation of identity lifecycle management will be critical for strengthening SOD enforcement in the years ahead. Many organizations still rely on manual provisioning and deprovisioning processes, leading to privilege accumulation, access creep, and compliance gaps. Automating identity lifecycle workflows ensures that users receive appropriate permissions at the time of onboarding, have their access adjusted when roles change, and are promptly deprovisioned when they leave the organization. AI-driven identity lifecycle management tools can dynamically adjust user permissions based on real-time risk assessments, ensuring that employees, contractors, and third-party vendors do not retain conflicting privileges that violate SOD policies.

Regulatory compliance will continue to shape the future of SOD enforcement, as governments and industry regulators impose stricter access control requirements. Regulations such as the General Data Protection Regulation (GDPR), the Sarbanes-Oxley Act (SOX), the Health Insurance Portability and Accountability Act (HIPAA), and the Payment Card Industry Data Security Standard (PCI DSS) mandate strong IAM practices, including SOD implementation. As regulatory frameworks evolve, organizations must ensure that their IAM and SOD policies align with emerging compliance standards. Automated compliance tracking solutions will play an increasingly vital role in simplifying audit readiness, generating access control reports, and demonstrating SOD adherence to regulatory bodies. Organizations that proactively align their SOD strategies with compliance requirements will reduce the risk of financial penalties and reputational damage.

The increasing reliance on third-party vendors, contractors, and business partners introduces new challenges for SOD enforcement.

Organizations must extend SOD policies beyond internal employees to cover external users who access corporate systems, data, and applications. Third-party risk management solutions integrated with IAM platforms help enforce SOD controls by applying strict role-based access policies, time-limited access permissions, and continuous monitoring of third-party activity. As supply chain security becomes a growing concern, organizations must ensure that vendors and external users do not accumulate excessive privileges that could lead to fraud, data breaches, or insider threats. Future advancements in vendor risk management platforms will further strengthen SOD enforcement by providing real-time insights into third-party access behaviors and risk profiles.

The future of SOD will also see greater emphasis on privileged access management (PAM) to mitigate risks associated with administrative users. Privileged users, such as IT administrators, security analysts, and finance executives, often require elevated access to perform critical tasks. However, granting persistent privileged access increases the risk of SOD violations, insider threats, and unauthorized system modifications. Organizations must adopt just-in-time (JIT) access provisioning, requiring privileged users to request temporary administrative rights only when necessary. AI-driven PAM solutions will enhance SOD enforcement by continuously monitoring privileged sessions, detecting anomalies, and revoking excessive privileges in real time. By integrating PAM with IAM platforms, organizations can prevent privilege escalation and strengthen SOD governance for high-risk users.

Security awareness and training programs will remain a key component of SOD enforcement in the future. While automation and AI-driven security controls enhance policy enforcement, human error remains a significant factor in SOD violations. Employees, managers, and IT teams must receive continuous training on SOD best practices, access control policies, and compliance requirements. Organizations will increasingly leverage AI-driven security awareness platforms that deliver personalized training modules based on user behavior, job roles, and risk exposure. Gamified training approaches, interactive learning modules, and real-time security coaching will further improve user engagement and knowledge retention. By fostering a security-conscious culture, organizations can reduce the likelihood of accidental SOD violations and ensure that employees play an active role in enforcing IAM policies.

As IAM continues to evolve, organizations must embrace a proactive approach to SOD enforcement that leverages automation, AI-driven insights, and adaptive security models. The convergence of Zero Trust, cloud-native IAM solutions, and AI-powered risk detection will redefine how SOD policies are implemented and monitored. Organizations that invest in modern IAM technologies, strengthen their compliance frameworks, and enhance security awareness programs will be better equipped to mitigate risks, prevent insider threats, and maintain operational integrity. The road ahead for SOD in IAM requires a commitment to continuous improvement, innovation, and alignment with emerging security trends to ensure that organizations remain resilient in an increasingly digital and interconnected world.

www.ingramcontent.com/pod-product-compliance
Lightning Source LLC
Chambersburg PA
CBHW071148050326
40689CB00011B/2027